STRING QUILTS

dedication

—

For people who want to make
something out of nothing.

STRING QUILTS

sustainable patchwork projects
using fabric scraps

CAROLYN FORSTER

SEARCH PRESS

Contents

___

Introduction

Sustainable, Sustainability

1: able to be used without being completely used up or destroyed.

2: involving methods that do not completely use up or destroy natural resources.

(Definition and Meaning, Merriam-Webster)

> "What we see depends mainly on what we look for."
> – John Lubbock

String quilts are a type of patchwork quilt that has come to epitomize economy and resourcefulness. By using up the very last scraps of fabric, or the very first scraps that we discard (when we neaten up strips or bolts on our cutting mats), we can create warm and comforting quilts from very little, just as makers have done before us.

More than ever we are becoming aware of how our daily choices can affect the bigger picture and our planet. We're now seeing words like 'sustainable' and 'sustainability' in discussions about sewing practice and making. And, as the quote left reads, some of us will see something to throw away, and others will see fabric that can be used. When we are questioning where our resources are coming from, our methods of production and how they affect our environment and well-being, we can learn a great deal from old quilts and the sewing practices involved in making them. With a little thought and ingenuity, we can play our part in making our quilts and quilting sustainable.

As quilt makers and patchworkers, we can look back at a long history of making useful, functional and beautiful quilts with what little resources the maker had available. 'String quilts', 'scrap quilts' and 'utility quilts' are all types of quilt that come to mind. These kinds of quilts have kept a practical, creative and often therapeutic textile craft alive and relevant over the centuries, and it would be great if it was something we could pass along to future generations too.

As with many things, quiltmaking goes in fashions and cycles. Be aware of this, and don't let practices that go out of favour get lost. Big-stitch quilting wasn't something that was 'acceptable' a few years ago, but it had been a go-to of previous makers in their utility quilts. Learning a wide base of skills allows you to be more creative and resourceful in your sewing.

Making quilts is not something only for those that can afford it; it is for everyone, and string quilts are ideal if you're keeping an eye on spending. By using materials you might normally throw away, you can stitch quilts more economically than you may have thought.

The techniques for making string quilts use basic skills. Although you will be using classic techniques, by stitching with randomly selected strings and scraps, you will be making creative, unique pieces.

There are ten quilts and five 'gifts and accessories' – smaller projects – to make and inspire you in this book, all made using the basic principles of string piecing. Several of the smaller projects can be made from the bits left over from quilts and quilt blocks, proving that you can always find ideas and creativity if you look in the right places.

I'm not saying all your quilts have to be made up entirely of leftovers, and not every quilt has to be a string quilt. But by taking a look at what you have before going out to buy more, being mindful of what you consume can become a creative and fulfilling part of the patchwork and quiltmaking experience.

history of string quilts

String quilts have always been a part of the American quilt-making tradition, but have not always survived to be studied and hung in museums or published in books.

Very much a utility quilt, which is made from scraps and for regular use, string quilts were not held in the same high esteem as the finely stitched special-occasion quilts. Because the latter were not used as regularly, or the circumstances that they were used in were more genteel, these quilts often survived for many family generations, sometimes ending up in museums.

String quilts have taken a while to come to the forefront of quilt studies, to be seen for the works of art that they are, and with the true spontaneity and resourcefulness in workmanship that they represent. However, with a greater awareness of Gee's Bend quilt makers, the popularity of improvisational techniques in modern quiltmaking, the desire for more sustainable practices, and thanks to collectors like the late Eli Leon and Roderick Kiracofe, old string quilts that have survived to the present day are now deservedly in the spotlight.

Due to the nature of these quilts, the provenance is mostly unknown. All were purchased through quilt dealers.

Clockwise, from top right: contained scrap quilt, c. 1880, unknown origin; classic Eight-point Star quilt, c. 1940s, originally in the collection of Jonathan J. Shannon; string Snowball quilt, c. 1930s, unknown origin; classic string block quilt originally made c. 1890s, which has then been pieced with sashing and posts c. 1970s, unknown origin; variation on the Eight-point Star quilt, c. 1940s, unknown origin; string Snowball quilt, unusually with a white background, c. 1940s, unknown origin.

The first string quilts I saw in books were in *Mississippi Quilts* by Mary Elizabeth Johnson (2001). One of the reasons for their name, in a definition given in this book, was that even the strings on aprons could be unpicked to be used in quiltmaking. The blocks were made on square foundations to stabilize the often narrow fabrics used for the blocks. One of the exciting things about these quilts then – and now – is that no two quilts were the same, since they were stitched with random scraps of fabric.

As we can see from the examples on these pages, many of the old blocks were pieced but not all ended up in quilts. Just like quilters today, sometimes the need to be doing with our hands overrides the need to actually finish something! Because the papers used for stabilizing the blocks are still in the backs of some of these unfinished pieces, we can quite accurately date them (se the example top-left). Many surviving blocks come from the 1930s, the era of economic depression.

String quilts have been around since the late 1800s, mainly in the southern states in the USA due to their poor economy. However, the Great Depression in the 1930s meant the practice of making these quilts spread more widely. Making warm bedding from very little came into its own during this time, primarily due to a scarcity of money and resources. Yet for some, especially for those living in rural communities, it was a continuation of a sewing practice they had always known. For others, it become a way to socialize with other women while doing something practical and at very little expense. Sayings from this time include 'Never waste a smidgen of material', 'If you can't be rich, be resourceful' and 'Use it up, wear it out, make it do or do without'. Making these string quilts was a homemade comfort when few luxuries could be afforded.

Top-left image: *part of a Snowball block. The strings have been sewn to old newspapers by hand. The maker has joined the string 'cores' to form a square with a hole in the centre. Perhaps they were appliquéing them onto a background. It is an unconventional approach to the block's construction, and perhaps this is why it was never finished.*

Middle-left image: *these star points have used fabric as the foundation, which will stabilize the fabric strips and add extra warmth in a quilt. Stitching to a foundation by hand would have made the work portable, and avoided the financial outlay of purchasing a sewing machine.*

Bottom-left image: *four string blocks sewn together. It is interesting that the fabric is sewn to the newspaper by hand, like the block at the top of this page (as is often the case), but it can't have been the nicest thing to handle while it was being worked.*

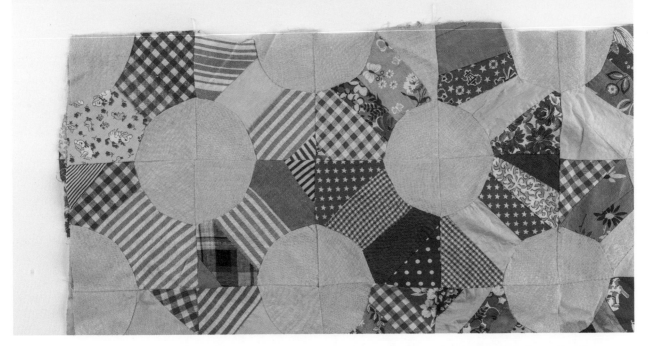

As the years progressed, many women were able to buy fabrics and kits to stitch a quilt, or wanted to buy ready-made bedding, so resourceful quiltmaking fell out of fashion until a revival around the 1970s and the American Bicentennial. When string quilts became of any interest again to makers, it came through the rightful recognition of the Black American quilt makers of Gee's Bend. Being in a cut-off rural area, using what they could get hold of and with no need to conform to fashions of the time, they had passed on their skills and resourcefulness through family members and developed a stunning use of colour and fabrics.

In the search for old string quilts, found examples have often turned up in various states of disrepair due to use and sometimes storage. String quilts have been found inside newer quilts, between bed springs and mattresses, and even covering old cars in sheds. As old examples of string quilts are often worn out or simply discarded, the ones that do survive are precious.

We can learn much from the practices of the makers who went before us: from the resourcefulness of their process to the excitement, vibrancy and spontaneity of the designs they created.

Top: *patchwork top of a string Snowball quilt (as it is not quilted). I've seen a lot of these quilts and it still surprises me how some of these blocks introduced the extra challenge of piecing the core first, as well as the need to sew curved seams.*

Bottom: *string pieced tulips (c. 1930s) and a diamond (c. 1880s). These were perhaps odd shapes that never made it into the quilts, or were left over from a finished quilt top.*

You will need

FABRICS

When I want to sew a new quilt – be it from a pattern or something I have designed myself – the fabrics are the key element to getting me started. If the fabrics aren't right in my own mind, then the project will be put on hold until the fabrics click with the design. That said, string blocks can be sewn with any pieces to hand, and fabrics that will bring the quilt together can be chosen when the blocks have been stitched. This makes string quilt blocks a great 'go to' when you want to sew, but perhaps don't have the final quilt in mind.

String quilts can be stitched solely with string blocks (see pages 46–55), but more often than not, other fabrics are incorporated. These fabrics can be from many sources, and it is worth thinking about these and how we can incorporate the ideal of sustainability in their use.

The fabrics that you use might depend on how you sew and quilt, whether by hand or machine. Different fabrics will be easier to handle in different construction methods, so bear this in mind when choosing your quilt.

your scrap bag

Many of my quilts start with the fabric in my stash. This is my go-to 'shop' if you like. Although having a stash at home is a great idea, for some it can become more of a fabric museum – rarely touched and mainly looked at! Make sure your fabrics are easily accessible when you need them, and store them in such a way that you can easily search for the right colour or print. If you can use up what you have already, then going to the fabric store to supplement your choices for the quilt becomes a more virtuous task. I know I've been guilty of going to my local quilt shop first, because it was easier to choose from there when my stash was so disorganized!

Take a close look at your fabrics and consider using them wrong side out, as sometimes this toning down of a design or colour is what is needed in your quilt. Consider over-dyeing the fabric if the overall colour is not what you are looking for, too. By using natural dyeing methods, you can be mindful of the environment while extending the lifespan of and adding variety to your stash.

quilt-making leftovers

Don't overlook patchwork blocks that might already be made, but have not yet found their way into a quilt. These can often be added to, or become the starting point of, a string quilt.

When you make binding tape, there is often some fabric left over. These can be saved and joined with other off-cuts for another scrappy quilt. Typically I cut my binding strips 2½in (6.5cm) wide, and these strips can be cut into narrower strips then combined to make string-quilt blocks. I also use these pieces for my thread savers (see page 17).

Excess backing fabric can also be saved. Usually I make my backing fabric 5in (12.75cm) larger all round than my quilt top, so I can use my quilt hoop right to the edge of the patchwork, and work with a neat edge when this is turned over a trimmed wadding/batting. Once the quilt is ready for binding, trim away the excess backing fabric and save the lengths in your scrap bag.

Similarly, any wadding/batting scraps can be held onto as these can be joined (see page 23) and used for 'stitch-and-flip' string blocks (see pages 29–33), or used as stuffing for other sewing projects.

Selvedges/selvages that have been trimmed away from newly bought yardage, in order to neaten up and straighten out the fabric's edges, can be salvaged and stitched together for a fun quilt string. See the Selvedge-edge Scrap Basket on pages 146–149 for an example of this.

your local quilt shop

The quilt shop may be your first port of call. If you have any preconceptions about purchasing new fabrics for your string quilts, it may surprise you to learn that many old string quilts show new fabrics were incorporated. The makers used scraps and strings to sew the main blocks then, once the design was finalized, yardage was purchased for sashing. Any left-over fabric from this would then go into the scrap bag.

If you purchase new fabrics for your quilt, your local and independent shop or store should be your first visit: it's worth supporting it because of the community it creates, and the classes and learning opportunities it offers. If your local quilt shop runs a loyalty scheme, sign up for that so you can take advantage of any regular discounts and offers.

When buying fabrics today, be aware of ethical, Fairtrade and environmental production practices. There are labels and trademarks that denote these better standards, OEKO-TEX® being one of the best known internationally. Keep an eye out for colours that could be used for multiple projects too, to make spending money worthwhile. For me, these are neutral cream and off-white prints. Often, the more you can buy of a fabric, the cheaper it can be.

Check out the sales for larger fabric pieces, and keep an eye out for over-runs and dead-stock fabrics too.

old clothes

Clothes that are no longer being worn but are not in a good enough condition to be donated can be saved for quiltmaking.

Be aware of any stains or frayed areas, and avoid cutting them out for patchwork. Note the fibre content too, as this can affect future laundering and ironing. Also, if the fabric is dense or has a high thread count, it might be hard to hand sew or quilt. If this is the case, make it easy on yourself and use these fabrics for machine-sewn projects. Salvage what you can in the way of buttons, zips, pockets, labels and thread for future projects.

It is worth noting that some of these clothes will hold sentimental value. Using a number of garments from one person can imbue that quilt with a very special meaning, becoming a memory quilt of that person or those times.

Charity/thrift/op stores are a good source for old clothes and household textiles, and they're always worth a browse when you are passing by.

If you make your own clothes, save the off-cuts for quiltmaking. This is the way many old quilts started out. Today, many quilters are turning to dressmaking having built up their sewing confidence, so don't forget the scraps leftover from your new-found skills to use for patchwork.

Why not even stitch garment labels together for a fun-looking coaster! See page 34 for more details.

household textiles

Vintage embroidered linens are often not used very much these days, and so can often be found in charity/thrift/op stores very cheaply, or found in linen cupboards at home or in a friend or relative's house. Check for any stained areas and then re-use the good parts in your quilts. The embroideries make fun fussy-cut patches, but could also be used to patch up darning holes. The hemmed edges make good garden string or gift ties too.

Old tea cloths and brushed cotton and flannel bedsheets should not be forgotten. Tea cloths can be used on the front of quilts and even sewn together to create a quilt back. This is a lovely idea if you have a collection of novelty towels collected from holidays, that now might not be used as they should. Brushed cotton flannel sheets can be used as thin wadding/batting in quilts, or even just for backing a patchwork top. These coverlets then will have a cozy cotton backing without the heaviness of a full wadding/batting. Sometimes, this is just what we need in warmer climates.

Curtains or heavy-weight fabrics can be used as quilt backings, again creating coverlets with no wadding/batting needed.

Moving ahead to foundations for our string piecing (see page 18), consider holding on to used tumble-dryer sheets if you use these: they work well as the foundation for string piecing.

community groups + charity sales

Look out for sewing, community or religious craft groups having swaps, or 'trash to treasure' tables at group meetings. Fund-raising jumble sales are worth keeping an out for too, as a way to boost your overall fabric collection.

THREADS

I use up a lot of my 'weird' colours when I string piece. These are spools that were bought for a one-time specific colour match, and now languish in the thread box. I don't worry about colour matching when seaming strings, but if you want to stick to neutral blending colours, then use these 'weird' colours for the bobbin. This means the top thread blends with your fabric, and the odd bobbin thread colour will be hidden on the back of your patches.

When buying thread, my usual mantra is to buy the biggest spool possible, and in neutral, toning colours. This way you save money in the long run, as large spools are often more economical and neutral colours can be used in lots more sewing projects too. You will also be using less plastic, as it takes less to create a large spool than lots of small ones. If you need a smaller amount of thread for portable stitching, then wind a bobbin from the large thread cone and take that with you.

If you have old threads that were thrifted or handed on to you, then use them by all means. If you can read the spool label, look for the weight and fibre content. Test the thread for strength too, as it can deteriorate over time. This will also help when considering fibre content: man-made fibres will stretch before snapping, and natural ones have less give. Pull the thread between your hands; if it snaps easily, don't use it for seams – keep it for tacking/basting, as it doesn't matter if the thread breaks for temporary stitches.

You can thrift thread from certain fabrics and clothes that often use strong thread, like jeans and cotton or paper sacks, by carefully unpicking the seams. The chain link stitching for these, if undone correctly, can be saved for tying quilts or wound around an old empty spool. I've saved the cords threaded through the top of a pair of curtains; these are great for tying quilts, which has been a common practice in quiltmaking since at least the 1930s.

◇ **50wt:** This is the most familiar weight of thread, and is often used on the sewing machine for piecing patches. It can also be used for machine quilting and adding texture, but its weight means it's not too visible.

◇ **40wt:** Slightly thicker than 50wt (as the numbers get smaller, the thread gets thicker), 40wt can be used for patchwork piecing but it also works well for machine quilting. It is my preference for hand finishing the binding on a quilt.

◇ **28wt:** I use this for hand piecing patches and for fine hand quilting, as I like the thickness of the thread – it seems to fill the hole the needle makes in the fabric.

◇ **12wt:** This is the thickest general thread I use, and it works well for anywhere you want a strong bold stitch (like big-stitch quilting), even on the machine.

◇ **Coton Perle:** This is an embroidery thread and comes in different weights. I use 12wt for big-stitch quilting; 8wt is great for tying quilts.

Thread savers

Being economical when sourcing thread is one thing, but when machine sewing there are ways we can use less. As well as being resourceful with your fabrics, think about how you use your thread on the sewing machine.

Lots of us are familiar with chain piecing in our quiltmaking, which saves us time and thread. But often when patchwork can't be made this way, we end up with blocks that need threads cutting away. Generally, all that thread is discarded and wasted.

If you use a thread saver, this isn't necessary, and you can make some fun textile pieces with these too. For those of you who have problems with the threads eating themselves when you start sewing, this method mitigates that.

When you come to the end of sewing your patch, block, binding or other pieces of fabric, and you need to sew another piece, rather than cutting the thread or chain piecing, take a piece of left-over fabric that's about 2½ x 2in (6.5 x 5cm) – often I use a piece cut from left-over binding – then fold it in half so it measures 1¼ x 2in (3.25 x 5cm). Place this in front of the presser foot as you finish stitching your patch then, as the patch comes out the presser foot, insert your thread saver. This is so the machine 'thinks' it's still sewing.

As you sew into the next, unstitched fabric piece, and when you're done with the thread saver, just snip the threads close to the thread saver. Pop it back under your foot when you finish up your final patch, so no thread is wasted!

discarding spools

If you are looking for ways to use up discarded plastic spools, you could tie them onto strings and hang them on fruit trees in the garden to deter birds, or keep them for children to play with for dolls-house, shop or counting games. You can also use them to wind thrifted threads from unpicked garments. If they come apart, use the bases as counters, or wind embroidery skeins around them instead of card. If you have old wooden spools these are again great for children's games or building blocks. But also, with four nails driven into the top, they are the classic French knitting loom.

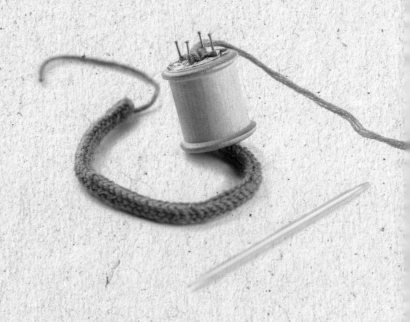

FOUNDATION CHOICES

One of the most common ways of stitching strips, patches and strings into a patchwork block, and the classic way that many string-pieced blocks were made, is on a foundation. You can see many examples from the past of paper foundations with fabric strips stitched to them, ready to be sewn into a quilt; you can even find whole quilt tops with the paper fragments still in place. Sometimes you can see a date on the newspaper, if that's what's been used as the foundation, which gives a very good idea as to when the block was made.

What you use as a foundation can depend on where you stitch the blocks, what you have available, and whether you are stitching by hand or machine. There are products you can buy to stitch on, or you can use what you have available. Think about the final quilt and how you want that to feel, as well as the actual process of stitching, as it is important to enjoy making your quilt.

newspaper

This is commonly seen in vintage and antique patchwork pieces that were never made into quilts; or, in some cases, quilt tops that were never quilted. From an historical point of view, these are fascinating insights. You can often still read the articles and dates, which fixes that stitching to a point in time. These old pieces were often stitched by hand.

Today we can still use newspaper, and personally I find it nicer to work with on the sewing machine than by hand. At the end, after the blocks are squared up and trimmed, the paper needs to be taken out. Sewing with a smaller than usual stitch on the machine helps this process as it perforates the paper.

paper

If you have old papers that are thin, and are the same weight as newspapers, then these can be used as foundations. Again, sew with a small machine stitch as you will need to remove the papers afterwards.

muslin/calico

Sewing the strings to a light-weight fabric foundation has the advantage that it can stay attached to the quilt top after it is sewn. This will make the seams slightly bulkier, so the quilt top might not need wadding/batting as there is already an extra layer of insulating fabric. A fabric foundation makes the sewing process by hand more comfortable than using paper. If your muslin/calico has a coloured pattern, you need to take care that it does not show through the strings.

The quilting would best be done on a machine, or the quilt will need to be tied, depending on the thickness of the overall sandwich – especially if wadding/batting is added.

In some string quilts, the muslin/calico isn't stitched over and is left exposed, making the foundation a part of the design; see page 33 for more on this.

thick fabrics

Sewing strings onto a heavy-weight fabric, such as denim from jeans or old curtains, means it will probably only need backing and no wadding/batting. Like muslin/calico (see above), it will stay attached to the quilt top. This type of coverlet quilt would be best tied too, because of how thick the layers will be, making for a quick finish.

sew-in, light-weight interfacing (such as L11/310 by Vlieseline®)

I started using the lightest weight of sew-in interfacing as I had some left over from garment making, but I also liked the idea that it could stay in the quilt without affecting the type of quilting I would do later. This is my most-used method, and many of the foundation-based string blocks in the book include it. Different brands may vary in their ability to be ironed during the stitching process, so make sure you sample your chosen interfacing before you start on your actual project.

tear-away interfacing

This is often used to stabilize fabric for machine embroidery, and comes in different weights. Tear-away interfacing would work for machine stitching the strings; that said, if you are using light-weight fabrics for your strings you will need to take care, as the seams can stretch due to the nature of the interfacing. Because of this, I'd recommend only using this foundation for strings made from heavy-weight fabrics.

As with the newspaper and paper foundations, and as the name suggests, you will need to tear out this foundation after trimming the blocks. So, as before, use a smaller stitch when sewing to perforate the interfacing.

soak-away interfacing

These foundations are designed to dissolve in water. You may be tempted to leave dissolving until the quilt is complete, but then the 'glue' may not fully come out and will be left trapped inside the quilt. If you treat each block independently, and soak each one as you make it, then you can make sure all the glue dissolves. However, this does add another step in your quiltmaking, as you will need to dry the blocks and re-press the seams. This approach might be workable, perhaps, for the odd one or two special blocks, but you will need to think about the soaking and pressing stages, and how it will work in the overall quilt-making process, before you start stitching.

EQUIPMENT + NOTIONS

It is easy to be drawn into buying the latest or most advertised gadget. But many of us, with too many gadgets, turn to the same trusty and useful piece of kit time after time. Here are a few of the things that I use a lot and the reasons why I think it is worth investing in them.

needles, pins + clips

Buy good-quality pins and needles. They will last longer than cheaper versions and be a pleasure to sew with. The more stitching you do, the more you will realize that the different needles and pins all have a job to do.

For hand piecing and hand-finishing binding, size 10 Sharps needles are my go-to. For big-stitch hand quilting I use size 6 Betweens or Embroidery needles.

Pin wise, patchwork pins are fine and are great for piecing; short appliqué pins are great for piecing as well as appliqué. For safety-pin tacking/basting, I use 1in (2.5cm) long safety pins; if you can get the ones with plastic covers, it will make the process easier on your hands. Using a teaspoon (or a grapefruit spoon) to help close the safety pins makes it easier on your hands.

Fabric clips work well for holding multiple layers together without distortion, and a mid-size clip will cover most tasks.

scissors

The two main types of scissors you will use are small scissors for threads, and larger fabric shears. Make sure what you use is comfortable in your hands. My favourite small scissors have large openings for your fingers, making them quick and easy to handle. Fabric scissors can often be heavy, and if this is a particular concern look for brands with extra features such as serrated blades. These will grip the fabric as they cut, making things easier for you, and still cut with a perfectly straight edge.

thimbles + finger protection

For quilting and some hand sewing, you will find it easier on your hands if you can protect your fingers with thimbles. It takes many of us a while to get used to these, and there are many products in the shops to help. Trying anything to protect your fingers is a good thing, but it can be expensive. Bear in mind that the goal is always to make your sewing practice more comfortable and, ultimately, if you can get used to using a durable metal thimble, like our great grandmothers, so much the better.

template materials

If the shape you need to cut out is one you will use a lot then it is worth investing in template plastic. Mark the outline with a fine permanent marking pen then cut it out with sharp household scissors. The plastic will keep its shape through multiple uses.

If the shape is only being used a handful of times then photocopying it (or tracing it off), gluing it to a firm piece of card (like a cereal packet) then cutting it out will be fine. A card shape like this will deteriorate over time as the edges get soft and less accurate, but for a few uses it is all you need.

fabric markers

Hera markers, tailor's chalk and soap slivers are all things that have been around for many generations, and there is a reason for this. They mark accurately and are economical to use. Think about trying these tried-and-true tools before buying disposable plastic pens and markers that leave chemicals on the fabrics.

sewing by hand

Lots of people say to me that they'd love to make a quilt, but don't have a sewing machine. If this is the case, remember that many of the old quilts you see and aspire to create were made by hand. So, if you don't have a machine, start your quilt by hand.

If you choose to sew blocks by hand, a basic hand-piecing kit will be worth the investment. I stitch with size 10 Sharps needles, 28wt cotton thread and with thimbles on my fingers. In addition to pins and scissors, a pincushion is always useful – if you'd like to make your own, see pages 158–161.

sewing machine

If you'd like to make your quilts on a sewing machine, and you decide to buy one, try to visit a shop and test out the machine before buying. A reputable shop will allow this and have staff on hand to advise you on the best machine for your budget, needs and intended projects. It is always worth asking about traded-in second-hand machines, too. These older machines are often excellent quality and offer incredible value. Even though I have a new sewing machine, when I teach I still do a lot of my sewing on an old machine that is purely mechanical. So much less goes wrong or breaks down on a mechanical sewing machine, and this is my go-to when all I need to do is a basic straight stitch.

You will find certain machine feet useful: a **¼in (5mm) piecing foot** is good for sewing patchwork pieces together, and a **walking (even-/dual-feed) foot** is ideal for stitching through multiple layers of fabric.

iron + ironing board/pressing mat

There are lots of irons to choose from, and it's best to keep in mind your needs. If you do a lot of classes then a small iron, often sold as a travel iron, is a good buy. The best irons are ones that heat up to a good temperature, have a steam feature and are comfortable for you to handle. Also look for makes that are more energy efficient, perhaps with an automatic shut off if you leave it on for long periods of time.

For ironing boards, some cutting mats come with a padded back for pressing, or you can buy them separately. Fold-away table-top boards are often a good idea, as they're light-weight and easy to store. I remember when I first left home, I didn't have an ironing board; I used a folded towel on a table – not perfect, but it did the job.

rotary cutter, rulers + mat

A basic 24 x 36in (approx. A1/600 x 900mm) mat, 6½ x 24½in (16.5 x 62.25cm) ruler and a 45mm lockable cutter are all you really need to make anything in this book.

However, some optional extras will make life easier. I use a 6½in (16.5cm) square ruler a lot for sizing up my basic blocks (see page 30), but you'll see later (see page 31) that you can square up with your long ruler too. If you do decide to invest in one square ruler I suggest buying the biggest one – such as a 12½in (31.75cm) square ruler – as it includes all the smaller sizes too. These decisions can make your sewing easier, and you may end up spending less than you think.

WADDING/BATTING

purchased

If you wish to buy wadding/batting for the projects in this book, you can. That said, I'd recommend looking for brands that use recycled resources and follow sustainable practices. These might include fibres from rapidly growing plants/fibre sources, like bamboo, or recycled fibres.

recycled

Have a look at what you have left over from finished projects – chances are you will have spare wadding/batting. If you tend to use one particular type or brand, pieces can easily be joined together to form a bigger piece.

Methods to join pieces include:

◇ **Sewing-machine zigzag stitch (A)**. Butt the edges of the wadding/batting then sew over the 'line' where the edges meet with zigzag stitch. Make sure your stitch is wide enough to cover the edges, and that the stitch is not too short: you do not want a hard line of dense stitching holding the wadding/batting together, as it can affect the drape of the quilt.

◇ **Hand stitching with baseball/suture stitch (B)**. Bring the needle up on one side of the wadding/batting, ¼in (5mm) or so away from the central gap. Bring the needle up on the other side, a little further along than your previous stitch so they're slightly offset. Repeat this motion of coming up alternately left and right; the stitch will evenly pull the edges of the wadding/batting together. Finish off with a few backstitches in the wadding/batting to secure.

If you don't want to use wadding/batting, then there are plenty of alternative fillings for your quilt. What you use will often depend on how the quilt will be quilted.

◇ **Wool blankets**. Old wool blankets add a lovely weight to a quilt, and great insulation too. Depending on the thickness of the quilt sandwich, use a utility quilting stitch (see pages 66–71) or hand tie (see pages 72 and 73).

◇ **Old quilts**. Controversial as this might sound, filling your quilt with a much older one was once not an uncommon practice. When a quilt became too thin or worn, or out of favour or fashion, in the past it could be recycled as the wadding/batting in a new quilt. It might not be to everyone's liking, but some think it's better to use a quilt in this way than to let it sit forgotten in a cupboard.

◇ **Flannel sheets**. If you want light-weight wadding/batting, old brushed cotton or flannel sheets work well. Often they are large enough for a quilt, and once quilted give the quilt a lovely texture without adding too much insulation.

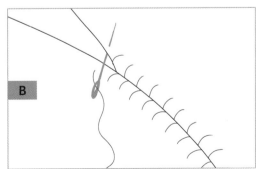

Cutting

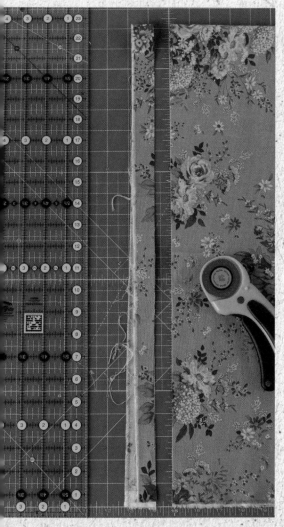

WHAT IS A FABRIC STRING?

A fabric string is a long piece of fabric that is wider at one end than the other.

Using strings in patchwork instead of strips, which are the same width across the entire length, will give your blocks a quirky feel. Because the widths vary and are unpredictable, there is the added bonus of not needing to worry about matching up the seams. You might not have given any thought to these pieces of fabric, and they are probably discarded. But, historically, lots of quilts were made using these pieces. Many of these were utility quilts, stitched for regular, daily use, but others like the work of Susan McCord (1829 –1909), a farmer's wife from Indiana, USA, elevated string-pieced appliqué to the next level with her meticulous design and sewing skills. If we are conscious about making the most of our fabrics, then it is worth keeping strings for our quilts and projects.

In the past, strings might have come about if dressmakers had odd shapes left over from cutting out pattern pieces. (And if you're a dressmaker, here's one way of using up those awkward long scraps!) However, today we are more likely to create them in our quiltmaking after neatening up the edge of the fabric. When we buy fabric, many of us will pre-wash it before using it. Once the fabric is washed, dried and pressed, when it comes to folding and lining it up on the cutting mat, there is often a misalignment of the raw edge once the selvedge is lined up. This uneven edge needs to be trimmed off (see the photograph left), ready to start measuring, so inadvertently you will have created a string.

That being said, I will sometimes deliberately cut a wider piece when evening up the fabric edge, so that the thin end isn't too narrow, to make it more useful and likely to be stitched into a quilt. If the small end of your string is narrower than ¾in (2cm), your string will be too thin to use: it will simply disappear into the seam allowance (SA).

CUTTING YOUR OWN STRINGS

If you don't have many strings in your scrap basket, there is no shame in cutting them from yardage or Fat Quarters that you have already. I tend to use a rotary cutter, ruler and mat for cutting, so these are what I've used for the technique below. However, fabric shears would work just as well for what we are aiming for here: a wonky line. We usually spend our time trying to line fabric up to cut straight and even strips, but for this you need not bother; we are looking for strings that are wider at one end than the other.

yardage

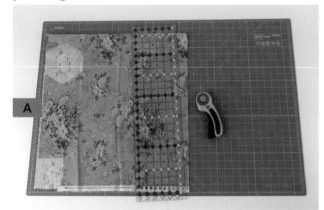 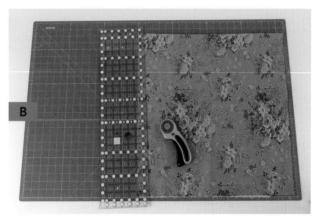

Place your fabric on the cutting mat, right side up and the selvedge edge along the bottom. Place your ruler over the cut end, at an angle (I aim for about ¾–1in / 2–2.5cm in from the raw edge at the top of the fabric) then cut from top to bottom. If you find the need to cut an even strip is too ingrained, try cutting from the other end of the fabric (**A**). Or, use the ruler back to front (so you can't read the markings so easily – see **B**) and use the plain side of the cutting mat, too, if you wish.

strips

If you have pre-cut strips either from purchased Jelly Rolls or from your stash, to make them into strings begin by splitting the strip in half, into two shorter strips. Keep the two pieces on top of each other (**A**). Place your ruler on top, angling it so you're about ¾–1in (2–2.5cm) in from the raw edge at the top of the fabric. Cut the fabric; you will now have four strings to play with (**B**).

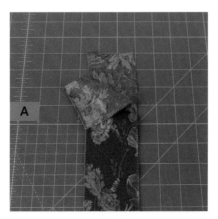 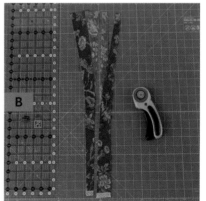

how to cut up a shirt

Shirts that have worn cuffs and collars often get discarded along with those that might be stained in areas. Sometimes it might feel that it's not good enough to pass on to a charity/thrift/op shop. However, shirts are a great source of fabric for your quilts. It is worth taking a few moments to consider how to cut and store them ready for sewing. If you don't have access to shirts in your household, then explore second-hand stores for those that have been donated. As you might not be going to wear it before cutting it up, shop for the largest sizes that you can, as these will yield the most fabric.

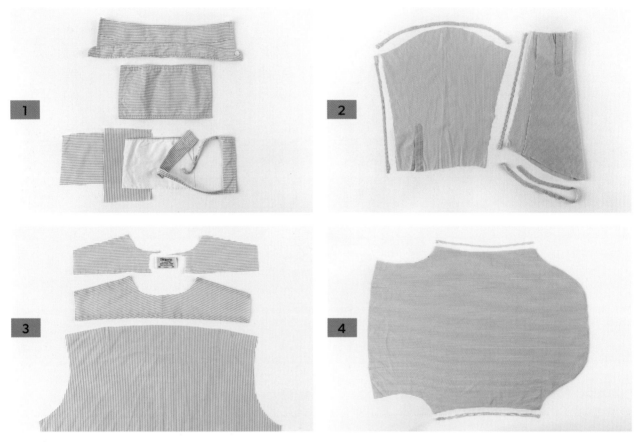

Step One Remove the cuffs by cutting above the seam. Although there will possibly be interfacing stuck to one of the fabrics, the other will be free and useable. Remove the collar by cutting below the seam. You can cut the collar apart as there will be fabric here to salvage too. If your cuffs and collar have buttons, remove these and set these aside before cutting up the collar and cuffs.

Step Two Remove the sleeves at the armholes. Cut each sleeve along the seam, and trim off the seam itself.

Step Three Cut the front and back of the shirt away from the yoke. If there is a label, unpick this. Set aside the yokes and label.

Step Four Trim off the side seams and set aside the back piece (this is the largest piece of fabric).

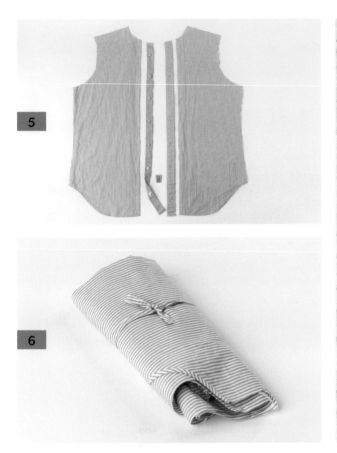

Tips

– If your cuffs have buttons, you could use the whole cuff to make a pouch for oddments. Simply fold it over to form a flap and stitch up the sides.

– Use long, cut-away seams for garden ties, or for anything else that needs tying up.

– If you leave the front button placket of your shirt attached, you then have the possibility of using the complete front as a pillow back (see pages 150–153). Or you can cut off the plackets, saving the one with the buttons. The buttons that were set aside from the cuff and collar can quickly be tacked/basted to this placket; that way a set of buttons is kept together in one place.

– If you have gathered enough unpicked labels, why not make them into a fun coaster (see page 34)?

Step Five Cut away the button and buttonhole plackets, just outside of the seam (although see also the third bullet in the tip box, above right). As with the cuffs, collar and yoke, salvage any buttons or labels.

Step Six Keep all the fabric together, ready to sew with. It can be tied in a neat bundle, using one of the cut-away seams. When the time comes to cut the fabric gleaned from this shirt, you will most likely end up with some strings from the evening-up process. Rather fittingly, as we have learnt, strings for quilts often started life in garment manufacturing, being the off-cuts from pattern cutting.

Piecing + sewing

BEFORE YOU BEGIN

◇ All seam allowances (SA) are ¼in (5mm) unless otherwise stated.

◇ All fabric cut off the bolt is cut across the width, unless otherwise stated.

◇ All fabric quantities are based on a 40in (101.5cm) useable width of fabric, bolt or yardage ('WoF').

◇ 'WS' means the wrong side of the fabric; 'RS' means the right side of the fabric.

◇ When machine stitching, set your straight-stitch length to 11 or 2.0 to 2.5, depending on how your machine is calibrated. It needs to be small enough to hold the fabrics together, but large enough to unpick easily, if the need arises.

◇ Press with a hot iron and a pressing pad or ironing board. Whether you use steam or not is up to you; some people think it distorts the work, but this hasn't been my experience.

◇ When pressing seams in one direction, I will press from the front. When seams need to be pressed open, flip your work and press from the WS, using the point of the iron to open the seam as you press.

◇ Take care to position the work and the seam you want to press correctly; you will then find you can press in one stroke.

* Pat Nickols, 'String Quilts', Uncoverings 1982, Vol. 3, American Quilt Study Group, pp. 53–57.

'STITCH + FLIP' STRING PIECING ON A FOUNDATION

Sometimes known as 'pressed-work technique'*, strings and strips of fabric are pieced together onto a foundation. A foundation is exactly what it sounds likes: it acts as a base for your patchwork pieces, keeps the fabrics supported and in a roughly uniform shape until the edges are trimmed, leaving a neat square of pieced fabric. It also helps keep all the bias edges on the outside of the block stable. In the past, these units or blocks could be readily stitched anywhere from a basket of scraps then, when enough were finished, they could be used in a quilt.

Historically, the units or blocks were often hand stitched onto a newspaper foundation, but that might not appeal to us today. You can substitute several foundations in the place of the newspaper (see pages 18 and 19 for foundation types) and sew the blocks on the sewing machine. Both hand-pieced and machine-sewn blocks can be combined in the same quilt.

Sewing the strings to a foundation keeps a focus on the shape you are making when stitching. You can select the right length of string for the seam you are sewing, cut a longer piece to fit, or join shorter pieces to the right length.

Tip

I often use 6½in (16.5cm) square foundations, and I have pre-cut squares in this size in my scrap basket ready for when the stitching urge strikes. It also helps keep the scraps under control, knowing that I can stitch at any time with no prep needed.

interfacing foundation

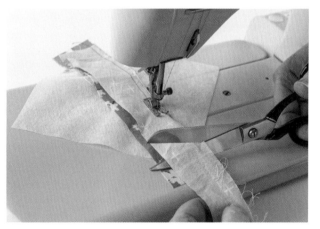

Step One Cut your foundation to the size of the finished block or patch plus the SA. I've cut 6½in (16.5cm) squares here, as my finished block size will be 6in (15.25cm). Lay a string of fabric diagonally across the square, RS up and so it roughly covers the centre of the corners. Don't line up the raw edge with the corners: you will end up with a seam line there, and this will make sewing the blocks together later a bit ungainly as you will have seams where more seams join.

Step Two Place the next fabric strip on top, RS down and with the raw edges aligned. Make sure the strip is long enough to overlap the foundation. Machine sew these two fabrics together, sewing through the foundation at the same time. Use your thread saver to start and finish (see page 17) or an automatic thread cutter on the machine if you have one, then cut away the excess strip.

Continued overleaf.

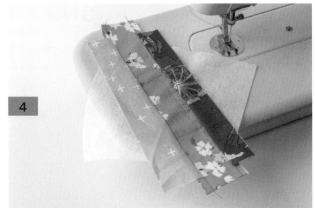

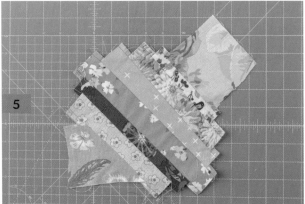

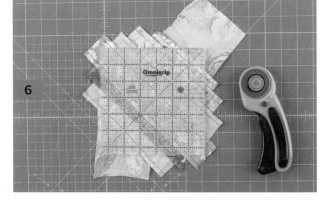

Step Three Fold the top strip away from the bottom strip then finger-press flat. Sew another strip to the other side of the central strip.

Step Four Now use the iron to press flat. Pressing after stitching a pair of strings before adding the next set gives a better finish.

Step Five Continue to add strips and scraps in the same way – working from side to side and pressing – until your foundation is completely covered in strips which extend over the edges. Remember, the fabrics are chosen randomly, and there's no need to make them match the next block. There will not necessarily be the same number of fabrics on each side of the central one, as it will depend on the shape and width of your fabrics. As you get close to the final corners, use wider strips or even triangles that are left over from other projects. **Note:** don't use really small pieces in the corners as these might either get trimmed off or become hidden in the SA and just create unnecessary bulk.

Step Six Once the final pressing is done, the block can be trimmed to its 6½in (16.5cm) square. There are two ways of doing this: using a square ruler or your standard quilting ruler. If you are using the latter, skip to step 7. For the square ruler, first flip the block so it is WS up, and you can see where the original foundation is. Place the square ruler centrally over the foundation. If you are using a 6½in (16.5cm) square ruler like I am, your foundation may likely be smaller than the original foundation; this is because the foundation can shrink up or distort slightly when you sew. It is does not matter, as we trim to the fabric not the foundation. Trim off the surplus fabrics. Turn the mat as you cut to trim safely and accurately. If there is the odd bit that looks big enough to re-use, stash it away in your scrap bag.

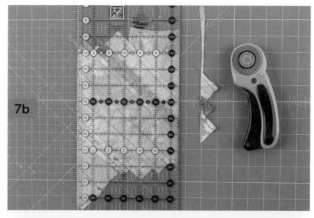

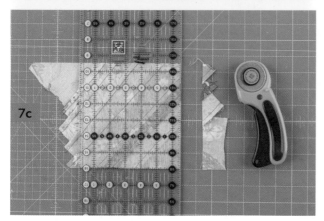

Step Seven If you are cutting with your standard long ruler, here is how to use it. Place the block on the cutting mat, WS up, line up the ruler with one side of the foundation, making sure the edge measures 6½in (16.5cm), then trim (**7a**). Turn the block and position the ruler so that it is 6½in (16.5cm) away from the trimmed side. Cut (**7b**). Rotate the block again so a trimmed side is sitting on a horizontal line on the cutting mat. Using the vertical line and your ruler, trim a straight edge (**7c**). Rotate the block once more, and again position the ruler so that it is 6½in (16.5cm) away from the trimmed side. Cut (**7d**).

Chain piecing string blocks

Once you are more familiar with the 'stitch-and-flip' process, try chaining piecing blocks. I usually work in groups of six blocks. Just feed in one foundation and a strip at a time, stitching down one long edge of each fabric strip, then cut the blocks apart when you have finished sewing. You can shuffle the order before sewing the next set, so you don't end up with the same fabrics always next to each other. This technique will save you having to choose and cut fabrics to length as your sew.

hand sewing 'stitch + flip' blocks

Making string blocks by hand is easier than you may think, and many old string blocks and quilts were made this way. Hand-stitched string blocks also make great portable sewing projects. All you need is a bag of scraps and some pre-cut foundations at the ready, and you are all set for some mindful hand stitching. I use 28wt cotton thread and a size 10 Sharps needle for hand sewing, as well as short appliqué pins.

Step One Place the first and second strip of fabric as you would for machine piecing, as shown on page 29. Pin the layers in place within the SA using some short appliqué pins, placing the pins at 1in (2.5cm) intervals.

Step Two Thread your needle with a length of thread as long as your arm and knot the end. Begin with a backstitch (this secures the seam) then start stitching the strips together through the foundation using small running stitches. Don't start stitching outside the foundation, as when it comes to trimming the block you don't want to be cutting through the stitching. At the next pin make a backstitch, again to secure the seam. Remove the pin. Continue sewing the rest of the seam in the same way, removing the pins as you sew.

Step Three At the end of the strips, when you run out of foundation, stitch three backstitches to secure the seam. Snip the thread, leaving a tail of about 1in (2.5cm), as shown. Finger press the flipped seam flat.

Step Four Continue to add strips in this way until the block is complete. Press it with an iron before trimming to size, as on pages 30 and 31.

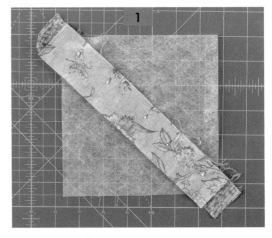
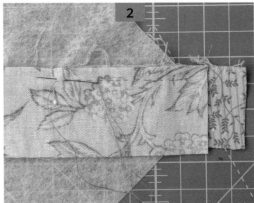
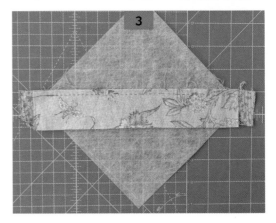

fabric foundation

This can be used in the same way as interfacing. Often the fabric is completely covered, so make sure it is not one with a pattern you'll miss; inexpensive light-weight muslin/calico is ideal. If you're using a patterned foundation, make sure the pattern does not show through on the fabrics that you'll place on top.

The foundation fabric can also be your 'centre' strip. Start stitching with the 'second' strip. Place this RS down, as per page 29. Depending on where you place this second strip, you can explore how wide you want the exposed foundation to be. Machine sew in place as before, then flip the 'second' strip so its RS is facing up. Finger-press. Do the same with the other side, then press with the iron. Continue with the remaining strips as before.

You can take advantage of the foundation and use it as part of the block design. In the same way that we add a consistent fabric down the centre of the Basic String Block quilt on pages 108–111, we can use the fabric foundation as a unifying feature.

selvedge string block

Selvedges are fun to add to string blocks, or even to cover a whole block, and you can use the words, colour dots and motifs in a meaningful way if you wish. I like to try to theme the colours or the words, especially if I am making coasters from these as gifts (similar to the one on page 34).

The method I use is slightly different to regular string piecing, as I find the selvedge a bit too thick to keep folding over to make a SA. I simply overlap the selvedge edges then stitch from the top, so the machine stitching is exposed and not hidden in the seam. If I'm making blocks entirely with selvedges, I use a 40wt thread (rather than the usual 50wt), as I find it gives the exposed stitches a little more durability. If they just feature in a string block, then I stick with the usual 50wt. In this picture, the wadding/batting is placed on top of the backing fabric (so both layers are treated as the foundation fabric) and the block is, in effect, quilted as it is stitched. You can use the method with a foundation fabric only.

I recommend starting and ending with a larger scrap of fabric that extends into the foundation by about 1in (2.5cm), and with the outside edges extending beyond the foundation too; this is to avoid too much bulk in the corners, which could be an issue when stitching selvedge blocks together. The last triangle is sewn in place using the regular 'stitch-and-flip' method.

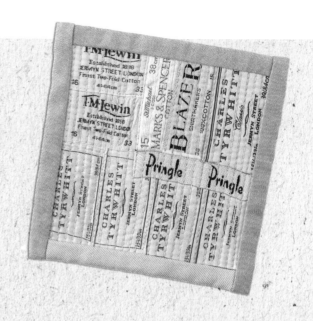

Label Coaster

If you need a project for the labels that you cut off and keep from the shirts, then this fun coaster is a good place to start.

MEASUREMENTS

4½in (11.5cm) square

REQUIREMENTS

Patchwork top:
Assorted labels from shirts and garments

Backing:
5½in (14cm) square of fabric from a shirt

Wadding/batting:
5½in (14cm) square

Binding:
Two 2½ x 5½in (6.5 x 14cm) pieces for the top and bottom, and two 2½ x 6½in (6.5 x 16.5cm) pieces for the sides – my pieces were cut from two shirt yokes

Notions:
Optional: fabric glue

Step One Remove any threads from the labels then press the labels flat.

Step Two Place the shirt fabric on a flat surface, WS facing up. Place the wadding/batting on top centrally. With the labels RS up, lay them over the wadding/batting in a pleasing way, slightly overlapping the edges. When you're happy, pin them in place or secure with fabric glue.

Step Three Halfway along the sandwich, and starting at one end, sew a line down to the other end using straight stitch on your sewing machine. Snip the thread, rotate your sandwich, shift it to the left or right, then stitch another line that's parallel to the first, using the width of the foot as a guide. Continue in this way, sewing back and forth, working from the middle to one side then from middle to the other side, until the coaster is covered and all the labels are secure.

Step Four Square up the stitched sandwich to measure 4½in (11.5cm). I left a small amount of excess wadding/batting around the outside edge, so the binding wouldn't encroach on the design of the labels too much.

Step Five Bind your coaster. The short pieces of fabric cut from the shirt's yoke work well when made into straight binding (see page 79), then added all around the coaster using the square-cornered binding method (see page 84).

STRING FABRIC

For this method you will produce a large piece of new fabric created from the strips you have sewn together. It is not on a foundation, so once it is cut it can be unstable at the edges. Use a smaller than usual stitch length on the machine when sewing this, so the cut edges don't unravel too much.

Once your new fabric is stitched you can decide how to use it. I cut sashing, framing and border strips from my string fabrics, which I then used in the Vintage Embroidered Tablecloths quilt (see pages 134–137) and the Tulips + Picket Fences quilt (see pages 128–133).

It can also be used in conjunction with stabilizers such as freezer paper and light-weight interfacing, both iron-on and sew-in; see page 41 for more on this.

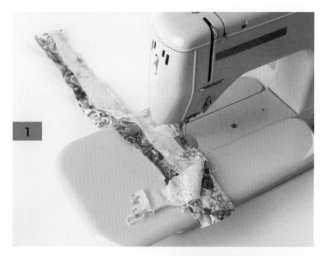

Step One Pair up your first two strips RS together, matching the straightest edges and a short end. Stitch from the matched end towards the other, as shown. Your strips may be of different lengths, so stop stitching when the paired seam runs out. I don't trim the longer end off; I like to leave it as my next strip could be longer and will pair up nicely. When it is trimmed off later, in the process of quiltmaking, it can go back into the scrap basket. Fold back the top strip so the RS of both strips face up.

Step Two Add as many strips as you need in the same way, until you feel you have a large enough area to cut from. I stitch the strings until I've made a panel that is roughly the same size as a Fat Quarter (20 x 22in / 50.75 x 56cm).

Step Three Press all the seams in one direction. If you want to, trim off the uneven strips, save them for other projects or for crumb sewing, which is when you use up even the smallest fabric scraps (see pages 76 and 77).

STRING LOG CABINS

These can be stitched from odd shaped strips and strings, and there is no need for the central patch to be perfectly square either. In fact, the middle of these blocks can be started with the off-cuts or crumbs from the strips and strings. Keep these pieces to one side and take a look at the crumb stitch experiments on pages 76 and 77 to give you ideas on how to use them. 'Waste not, want not' means down to the very last fabric scrap!

String Log Cabin blocks can be stitched by hand or machine, both with successful results. The blocks do not need a foundation to stabilize the strings or to achieve the finished shape. They are stitched with fabrics roughly cut on the straight grain, so won't have the bias edges that a basic block has.

The string Log Cabin blocks in the Vintage Crumb Log Cabin Patchwork quilt on pages 90–95 and the Half Log Cabin quilt on pages 112–115 are sewn and then trimmed and squared up. This method makes it easier to sew the blocks together for the patchwork top, and there's little precision involved in their making.

Half Log Cabin Quilt (see pages 112–115).

What fabrics should I choose?

As far as fabric selection goes, you can try to keep to similar width fabrics on each circuit round the centre patch, but again this does not really matter. The more differences in width, the more interesting the block will look.

I tend not to keep to the classic half-light, half-dark shading of the block either; call this improvisation if you will, but to be honest I tend to have fewer fabric scraps that I would consider 'light' in colour, so it makes sense to use what I have the most of. In the Half Log Cabin quilt I have gone with a half-light, half-dark colour scheme, as the pattern needed more definition. As always, it is up to you to use what you have.

Tips on stitching Log Cabin blocks

– If you are working on one block at a time, press the seams as you go with a seam roller or by finger-pressing, then use the iron at the very end. This saves time and energy (both electricity and yours!).

– If you are sewing a lot of blocks, chain piecing style (see page 31), you can press a whole batch all at once.

– Use the cutting mat when you finger-press or roll each seam, to help stabilize the fabrics. The mat will also help you check the size of the block as you sew.

– Use wider fabric strips for the outer edges of the block if you can, as you get towards your desired block size. This will mean that, when you square up the block, you will not be trimming too close to a SA. If the strips are too narrow, there's a chance the SAs will get caught in the seams when the blocks are joined together, creating more bulk.

classic log cabin

Step One Start with a piece of fabric for the centre of your Log Cabin block, making sure it's roughly square or rectangular. Stitch another fabric to one side, RS together. Fold back the second strip. If it's too long, you can either trim it to the size of the centre patch, or you can chain piece several centre patches to the second strip then cut into multiple centre patches (see the tip box on page 38). Here, I have simply trimmed the second strip.

Step Two Sew a third strip to the ends of the previous strip and the side of the centre piece (one straight seam), RS together. I'm working in a clockwise direction, but you could work anti-clockwise if you prefer. If the third strip is longer than necessary, as with the second strip you can chain piece or fold the strip where it's in line with the edge of the block, then cut away the excess with scissors.

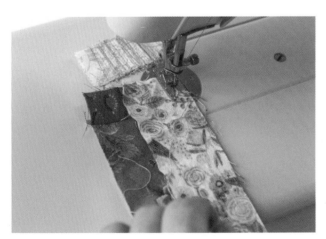

Step Three Add a fourth strip as before, attaching it to the previous strip and to one side of the centre panel, RS together. Fold back the strip so its RS is facing up.

Step Four Add another strip, RS together, to complete the first circuit. Press.

Continued overleaf.

Step Five For the second circuit, lay a strip over the second strip you added and sew RS together. Continue to add strips for the second circuit in the same way as the first.

Step Six Continue to add circuits until you achieve your desired size, pressing after each circuit. With each circuit, you will see the shape of the block changes depending on the width or straightness of each strip. Usually I recommend working in either a clockwise or anti-clockwise direction, but if you think you need to add a strip to a different side to square up your block, go ahead; it will be fine. It might turn out that the centre fabric is no longer in the centre; again, that's fine. To finish, square up your finished block, as per pages 30 and 31.

Chain piecing Log Cabin blocks

Like the 'stitch-and-flip' string blocks (see pages 29–33), you can chain piece three to four Log Cabin blocks. If you're new to this method, I recommend chain piecing after the first two circuits are established, so there is more fabric to work with and there's the added stability.

Simply sew a very long strip to one block then, as you reach the end, slide another established second block under the presser foot and carry on stitching. At the end, cut the blocks apart.

half log cabin

This block is a variation on the classic Log Cabin but, as the name suggests, it has a design that's only built up on two sides. To construct the block you start by adding a strip to one side of your starting square or rectangle, the next strip to the top, then repeat. The first side usually ends up requiring the least amount of a particular fabric colour as the strips are shorter than those added to the second side. Since I tend not to have many strings in lighter colours, I use this knowledge to my advantage and take a half-light, half-dark colour scheme approach, with the lighter colours used for the first side; this means I can fully make use of what I have.

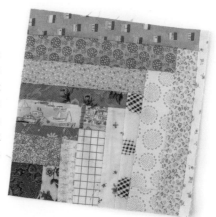

Completed half Log Cabin.

Step One Start by stitching two pieces together as per step 1 on page 37. Press the seam. As I'm opting for a half-light, half-dark scheme, I've added a light-coloured strip to the right of my darker-coloured centre piece. I've chosen the classic red for my centre (historically, it represents the hearth of the home). Press the seam of the second strip (the lighter strip, in my case) away from the centre piece.

Step Two Stitch a third strip to the left side of the two joined patches, as per step 2 on page 37. I have used a darker-coloured strip.

Step Three Sew a fourth strip to the second and third strips as shown, RS together, then press flat. I've used a lighter strip.

Step Four Continue in this way, sewing strips to the two previous strips and alternating light and dark colours, until your block is the desired size. Make sure to keep the ends of the strips that will be on the outside edge of the block slightly longer, just by ⅛in (3mm) or so; you do not want your block to shrink up on these edges or it will be uneven.

Step Five If need be, square up your block with a rotary cutter, cutting mat and ruler – I like to use a square ruler that's the same size as my desired size (in my case, 12½in or 31.75cm square). To square up, match the corner of the ruler with the corner of the centre patch, then trim the outer edges. Rotate the block, realign the ruler then trim off the remaining uneven edges.

Appliqué

Essentially, appliqué means stitching down patches of fabric, in varying shapes, onto a larger piece of fabric to form a picture or pattern.

Old quilts with string appliqué are not uncommon. Several vintage quilts feature appliqué motifs – one of my favourites is a 1930s quilt with tulips (which inspired the quilt on pages 128–133) – and in my old block and quilt collection there are tulips made from strings (see page 11). Appliquéd motifs are excellent for making use of very small scraps and strings in your fabric stash.

USING FREEZER PAPER

I've used freezer paper in two ways – for piecing and for appliqué. Using freezer paper for both methods allows you to work accurately with unusual shapes, whether they're diamonds for the Blue String Stars quilt (see pages 102–107), or curved shapes such as the petals for the tulip in the Tulips + Picket Fences quilt (see pages 128–133). The freezer paper also stabilizes the shape when sewing. With the piecing method, the freezer-paper shapes can often be reused several times; for the appliqué method, the freezer paper backs the fabric shape and acts as both an adhesive and stabilizer, and often tears when removed.

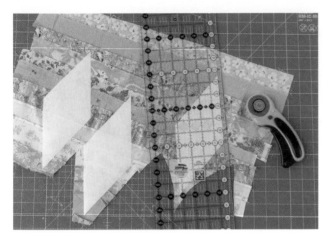

for piecing

Step One Cut the freezer paper to the finished size, then iron the shiny side to the WS of the fabric. I've ironed mine to the WS of string fabric (see page 35). If you're cutting out multiple shapes from freezer paper, and ironing them to the same fabric, make sure you leave enough space in between them – at least ½in (1.25cm).

Step Two With a rotary cutter and ruler cut out the shape, adding a ¼in (5mm) seam allowance all around.

Step Three The freezer paper should stay stuck to the back of the fabric while you stitch the SAs together on the machine, to keep the raw edges of the fabrics in place. When you finish sewing the block, the paper can then be pulled away.

for appliqué

Step One Cut and adhere the freezer paper to the back of your chosen fabric, as per step 1 for piecing (see left).

Step Two Cut out the shape (either with fabric scissors or a rotary cutter and ruler), adding a scant ¼in (5mm) SA. Experiment with the SA, as appliqué generally needs only a scant ¼in (5mm) or even ⅛in (3mm) SA. If your shapes are being cut from string fabric, the seams from piecing the strings may mean you need to make the SA more generous.

Step Three Turn under and tack/baste the SA to the WS of the paper shape. The tacking/basting stitches will be removed once the shape has been stitched in place (see pages 44 and 45).

INTERFACED APPLIQUÉ

This works very well at stabilizing appliqué shapes that you want to use in conjunction with the 'sew-then-turn-through' technique, and adds a relief effect to your appliqué shapes. The technique works best with bold regular shapes like circles, hearts and simple leaves. The shape demonstrated here is cut from string fabric (see page 35), but you could use this method for unpieced fabric too. You can use iron-on or sew-in interfacing, and the most successful results come from using the lightest weight interfacing; I've used sew-in interfacing (L11/310 by Vlieseline®) for the steps on this page. The Tulip Table Runner on pages 154–157 features interfaced appliqué.

Step One Trace your finished shape onto the interfacing and cut it out, adding extra for a SA. I often draw rounded shapes onto squares of interfacing cut 1in (2.5cm) larger than my finished shape; this allows for ease of working. Place the interfacing on the RS of the fabric. If using iron-on interfacing, note the sticky side should face the RS of the fabric.

Step Two Sew all around the outline on the machine, overlapping the stitches at the start and finish. If you are using shapes with points, always start and finish on the straightest edge.

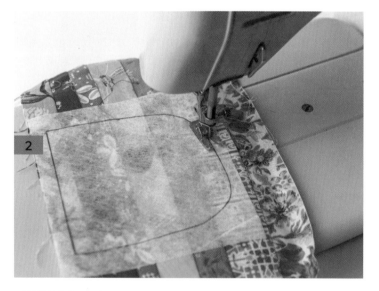

Step Three Trim the fabric and interfacing, leaving a scant ¼in (5mm) SA, then cut across the corners to remove bulk.

Step Four Carefully cut a slit in the centre of the interfacing, without cutting into the fabric, then turn the shape out through this hole.

Step Five Using a wooden point turner or something similar (wooden chopsticks are good), smooth the sewn edge from the inside.

Step Six Press gently (unless it is iron-on interfacing), as shown, then pin in place, ready to hand or machine stitch to your quilt top or other project. If using iron-on interfacing, you can only press these shapes when they are positioned on the fabric, as this will then stick the fabric shape in place. You will still need to secure the shape with hand or machine stitching.

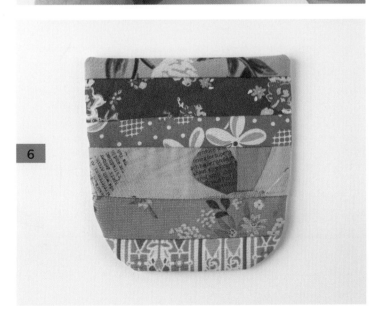

SEWING APPLIQUÉ SHAPES IN PLACE

The stitch I use for sewing on appliqué shapes is known as appliqué stitch or slip stitch. I use the same stitch to secure the bindings on the back of a quilt (see pages 80–85). Use a sewing thread that coordinates with or matches the fabric you are stitching down, and cut a length of thread as long as your arm for ease of stitching.

Step One Pin the shape into position on your quilt.

Step Two To start, bring the needle from the back of the shape up through the front edge, to hide the knot. Take it down through the background fabric only, close to the spot where the needle came up.

Step Three Take the needle up through the appliqué shape again, a little further along the edge. Pull the thread through, making a tiny stitch over the edge of the shape. Repeat almost all the way round the shape. If there is a paper template to be removed, stop 1in (2.5cm) from the start.

Step Four If needed, remove any tacking/basting stitches.

Step Five If you've used a template, remove it by pulling it through the gap with your fingers or tweezers.

Step Six Stitch the opening closed as before. To fasten off, leave the needle on the back of the work and stitch two to three stitches on top of each other through the background fabric only, in an area hidden behind the appliqué shape.

Appliqué shapes on the Tulip Table Runner (see pages 154–157).

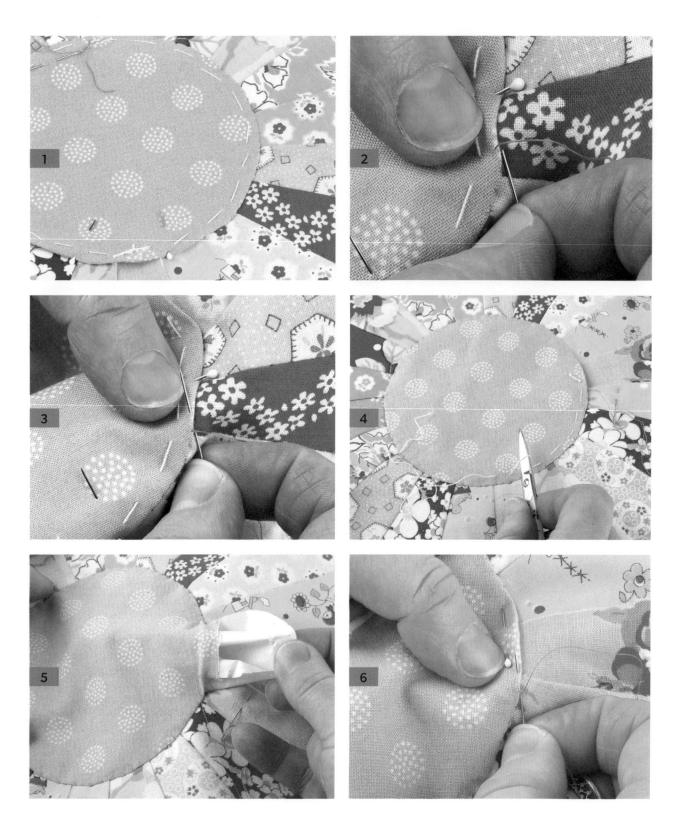

basic string block designs

I usually stitch string blocks with no particular quilt in mind. When they're made, it's fun to start playing with them and see the different layouts. The blocks can be stitched together with each other or grouped into fours and stitched with sashing; really, the possibilities are endless.

WHAT HOLDS A STRING QUILT TOGETHER?

By this, I don't mean the stitches and the quilting! I mean what makes the mishmash of leftover fabrics that become patchwork blocks look good together.

If you were given Fat Quarters of each fabric found in a string block and told to sew them together into a design, it would be hard. You may find no design or colour 'cries out', and the colours may seem like they won't go together.

But string quilts *do* work, often because there are so many blocks made from a mishmash of fabrics that they harmonize with each other. Indeed, often the blocks form a design of their own that takes you away from the fabrics, and draws you to the bigger picture that they create.

Here are some tricks you can use to visually hold the blocks together, if you're struggling to start off your design.

◇ To calm down busy blocks that feature lots of patterns, **use solid blocks** in between, ideally the same fabric. Yes, this is your chance to use up yardage that has languished in your stash, although you could go out and buy new fabric for this purpose.

◇ **Use a solid or neutral as part of the design**. In the Stars + Spiders' Web quilt on pages 122–127, the off-white fabric in the block and the border 'cleans up' the look of the quilt and makes it look light and fresh.

◇ **Add a border** around the patchwork top that pulls all the colours together. This is often going to be a busy print too, but the colours should coordinate with those in the blocks. The String Snowball quilt on pages 96–101 is a good example of this. This is also your chance to have fun shopping for more fabric, if necessary. Support your local quilt shop by taking your quilt top in and choosing a fabric for the borders.

◇ And if you have used up oddments in a border, buy yourself some **coordinating fabric for the binding**! Using what we have makes us feel good, and there is no harm in treating yourself and the quilt to a little retail therapy as a reward. You may even inspire some other quilters to do the same.

◇ **Use a common colour as part of the design**. In the Wonky Squares quilt on pages 116–121, navy-blue print fabric has been used alongside a white print fabric. It's not always the same print, but they are all navy. By avoiding using navy in other parts of the block, this acts as an anchor for the squares that you see.

◇ The quilting design plays a big part too. Choosing **quilt designs that are all over**, and not singling out a particular part of the quilt, will help give the quilt a homogeneous look.

BASIC IDEAS

Here are a few to get the ball rolling:

◇ Combine string blocks with plain squares (**A**).

◇ Strings can face in the same direction (**B**).

◇ Strings can point inwards, forming a large X-shape (**C**)…

◇ … or outwards, forming large diamonds (**D**).

◇ Strings can be rotated to make chevrons (**E**)…

◇ … or rotated to make miniature diamonds (**F**).

FOCUS COLOURS

Basic blocks can also be sewn with a feature or focus colour – such as the blue in illustration **G**. This can help bring a unifying element to the blocks and the designs they create. If scrappy isn't something that sits comfortably with you, then this element brings a calming effect. The Basic String Block quilt on pages 108–111 is a good example of this. Making the corners the same colour can also add harmony to scrappy blocks – see illustrations **H** and **I**.

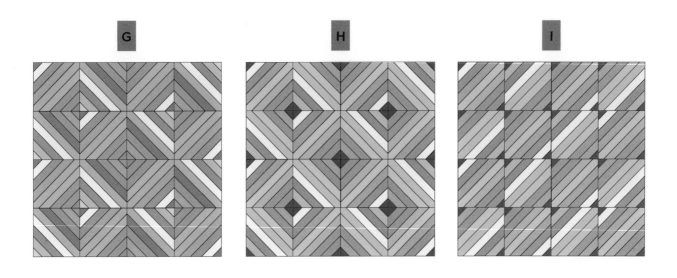

G

H

I

LIGHTS VS. DARKS

Another way to organize the fabrics in a scrappy block is to divide them into lights and darks (**J**). Whichever strip is down the centre of the diagonal will give the dominant look to the quilt. In the case of illustration **K**, the light fabrics dominate as they frame the dark strings.

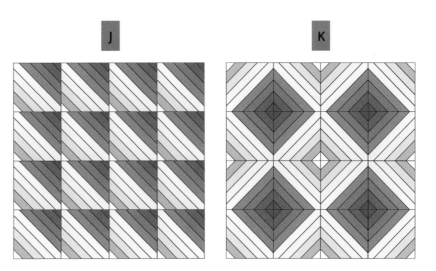

J

K

BASIC STRING BLOCK DESIGNS

HALF SQUARE TRIANGLES: PLAIN

After your string blocks are stitched, you can combine them with a plain or unpieced square of fabric and make Half Square Triangles (HST). Here I cut my squares to 6½in (16.5cm) square; I'll then use the finished 6⅛in (15.5cm) squares for the quilt. If you want to square them to a more logical size, such as 5in (12.75cm) or 6in (15.25cm), then do so; however, if you are just going to use them all in one quilt top, consider whether it is worth taking the time and creating off-cuts.

Step One From the plain/unpieced fabric cut a square the same size as your string-pieced block. On the back of the fabric square draw a diagonal line from corner to corner with a fine sharp pencil. Place the plain and string fabric squares RS together, making sure that the diagonal line 'cuts' through the strings and is perpendicular to them.

Step Two Stitch a ¼in (5mm) SA either side of the drawn diagonal line.

Step Three Cut along the drawn line.

Step Four Open out the new squares and press away from the pieced fabric. You now have two HST units.

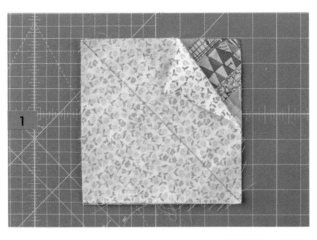

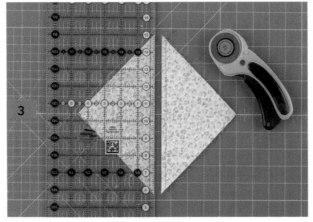
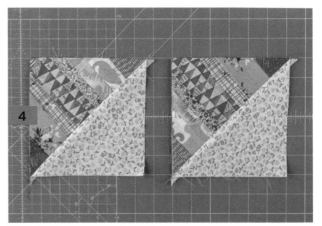

There are many layout possibilities with this design – see samples **L** to **Q** below for some ideas.

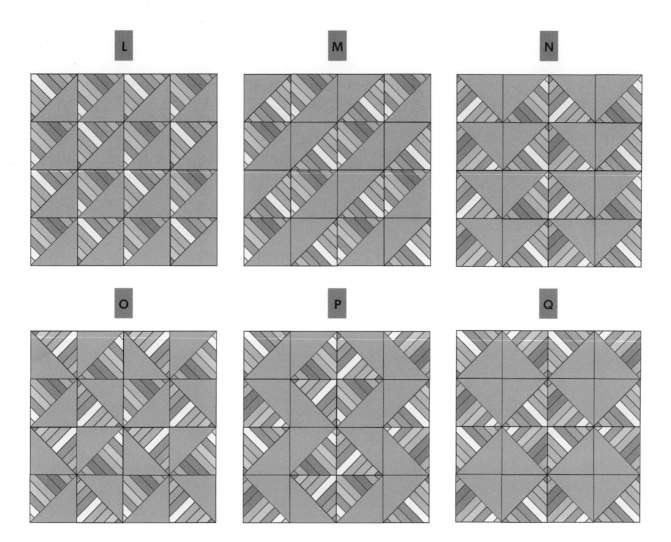

HALF SQUARE TRIANGLES: STRING STYLE

Another fun way to create this HST-type block is to sew it with strings.

I have used an 8½in (21.5cm) square foundation for this, as it is less fiddly to work with and suits the size and length of many of my string pieces. I start by sewing the light fabrics, so that when I start with the dark fabrics, they will cover the ends of the strings. If you sew the light strings second, there is a chance that the dark ends of the fabric will show through.

A square ruler is useful for trimming these blocks. The diagonal markings make it easy to keep the sewn diagonals in place and the block square. The square ruler should be either the same size or larger than the block.

This block is stitched in two parts – one half (or triangle) is stitched with the strips parallel to the diagonal, and the other half/triangle has the strips perpendicular to the diagonal. By stitching the strips in place on one side of the first triangle from the inside outwards, then the strips on the other side of the triangle from the outside edge to the centre, you avoid a chunky seam in the middle of the block.

Step One Cut out the square foundation and on it draw a diagonal line from corner to corner. Start with the light fabric strings. Place one string in the centre, on one half/triangle of the square, perpendicular to the drawn line and with one short end overlapping the drawn line by about ¼in (5mm). Place the second string on top, RS together, and stitch along the right-hand raw edges of the strips, from the inside to the outside edge. Fold the fabric open by finger-pressing or using a seam roller. Repeat to fill in this half of the triangle.

Step Two Now fill in the other half of the triangle. Stitch the next string to the left-hand side of the central strip, stitching from the outside edge and finishing at the drawn line. Continue to add strips in the same way until this half of the triangle is covered in strips that extend over the edge. You do not need to worry about neatening threads or reinforcing the beginning and end of each seam, as the lines of stitching in the middle of the foundation will be covered with a perpendicular seam later.

Step Three Place a string of dark fabric perpendicularly on top of the light fabrics, RS together and with one long edge matching the ends of the strings in the centre. This edge, like the light fabrics, should extend over the drawn line, as this is the SA. Pin. Carefully flip over the foundation, holding the dark string in place, then stitch along the drawn line from the back of the foundation, as shown. Stitching from the back means you can see the drawn line clearly as you sew.

Step Four Flip the foundation again, so the RS of the light strings are facing up. Open out the string of dark fabric then place a second dark string over it, RS together and matching the raw edges that sit over the empty half of the foundation. Sew, flip open then press.

Step Five Now continue to fill the second half with strings in the same way.

Step Six Once the foundation is complete, square up and trim off the excess fabrics, as on pages 30 or 31.

As with the other string-pieced blocks, there are many ways to use these HST string blocks.
Samples in illustrations **R** to **T** are some ideas to get the ball rolling.

PERPENDICULAR TRIANGLES

Similar to the HST, you can add a small corner of consistent fabric, perpendicular to your strings (**U**).

Draw a diagonal line on the wrong side of one 3in (7.5cm) square scrap, place it over one corner, RS together, then sew along the line. Trim ¼in (5mm) from the sewn line, through both layers, then press towards the added fabric. Illustration **V** shows another layout option.

Adding two perpendicular squares creates a hatchet or canoe block (**W** and **X**). If you save the cut-off corners from trimming, you have tiny HST blocks to play with (**Y**)!

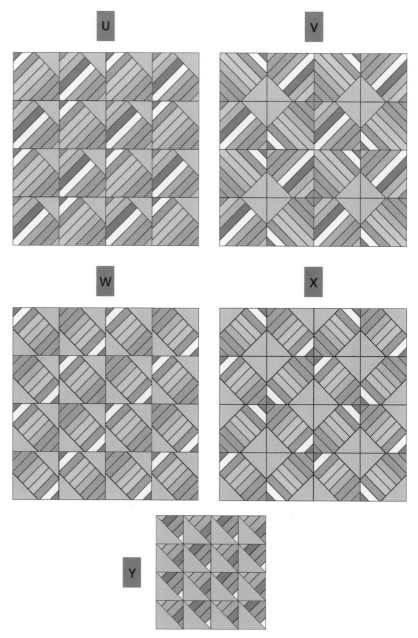

CUTTING OUT SECTIONS

Vintage string quilts often have the basic block with some elements cut away. A popular choice was cutting a quarter circle from two corners, making Snowball blocks as seen in the top quilt on page 11 (see also illustration **Z**). Another arrangement with two cut-out quarter circles can be seen in illustration **AA**.

If you cut a quarter circle from just one corner, you can make a sunburst block (**BB**) or a zigzagging design (**CC**).

Below: *String Snowball quilt (see pages 96–101).*

Layering +
tacking/basting

In preparation for layering and tacking/basting the quilt, press the quilt top and backing fabric. If you can, leave them somewhere flat so that they will not need a second pressing – draping both over a spare bed or stair rail is ideal. Unfold the wadding/batting the day before, to allow it to relax so that any creases can fall out. If you leave the wadding/batting in a steamy bathroom overnight, this also works well.

HOLDING THE LAYERS TOGETHER

By trying the different methods on the following pages, you will find one that suits you and your quilt; often this will depend on the quilt in question.

Generally, for all methods of tacking/basting, the securing method should form a grid (see page 59). This grid is often dictated by the patches in the quilt. There should not usually be a gap bigger than 6in (15cm) between the tacking/basting lines – about the size of your spread hand. If the patchwork does not have a grid to follow, again use your hand span as a guide.

Think about the way that the quilt will be quilted before you tack/baste it. Depending on the way that you quilt, you may not even need to tack/baste the layers together. For example, if you use a stand-up traditional frame with rollers, this will eliminate the tacking/basting process completely. Consider this option if you have the space at home and enjoy hand quilting in one particular place, as these are not easy to shift from one room to another!

If you use a circular hoop then safety-pin tacking/basting (see page 60) might not be the best choice. This is because the pins tend to get in the way of the hoop and need moving every time you reposition the hoop. If you are happy to keep doing this, then go ahead! It bothers some people but not others, but it is worth being aware of this before you start.

When you lap quilt, you do not have the additional stability that a hoop gives so a little denser tacking/basting will help to stop the layers shifting. For lap quilting, think about tacking/basting perhaps every 4in (10cm) rather than 6in (15cm). Use your closed fist as a gauge between tacking/basting lines, rather than a spread hand.

HAND TACKING/BASTING

Hand tacking/basting a quilt gives you the best control over the layers of the quilt and does not add any extra weight or bulk. Tack/baste the quilt in rows that are 6in (15cm) apart. You could use specialist tacking/basting thread for ease; however, think about using old threads that prove too weak to use for general stitching. Tacking/basting thread is generally a thread that is easily breakable between your fingers, so any weak threads will be well used here.

regular hand tacking/basting

◇ Start with a knot and a backstitch, then work running stitch from right to left on the quilt (left to right if you are left-handed). The stitches should be about ½in (1.25cm) long and evenly spaced (see the diagram below; the dashed lines indicate the thread and stitches below the fabric). Finish with a backstitch to keep the thread secure.

◇ As the needle and your hands are always on the top of the quilt, your fingers can get sore as the needle pushes up against them. Using a teaspoon or a grapefruit spoon helps ease the needle up through the layers, and makes the process quicker. As you take the needle through the layers, simply push the needle up against the edge of a teaspoon or grapefruit spoon (see image below right).

tailor tacking/basting

◇ Some people find the action of tacking/basting uncomfortable, as the needle is held horizontally to your body. If this is the case for you, try tacking/basting diagonally, known as tailor tacking/basting: the needle is held so it points towards your body, which can feel a more natural position.

◇ To tailor tack, thread the needle with tacking/basting thread and knot the end. Work the stitch from right to left (left to right if you are left-handed). Create rows of ½–1in (1.25–2.5cm) long diagonal stitches, depending on the length of the needle (see the middle diagram below). Finish with a backstitch.

Tacking/basting tips

– Use a clear, flat floor to lay the quilt flat. If you don't have the space, you can use community and church halls – just make sure to book the space when you know the cleaner has just been! This saves you having to move your own furniture around to make room for the quilt on the floor.

– For any tacking/basting done on the floor, consider using a kneeling mat or knee pads to cushion your knees.

– Using a carpeted floor will stop the quilt moving too much. The edges can also be secured with masking tape.

– Use large tables if kneeling on the floor is not an option. Community and church halls often have these, if you don't have one at home.

– Use the services of a long-arm quilter: many offer a tacking/basting service, which lets you sit down and enjoy the quilting. This thread-tacked/basted method offers all the advantages of manageability and no added weight, but with someone else having done the work.

Regular hand tacking/basting.

Tailor tacking/basting.

Using a teaspoon.

TACKING/BASTING SYSTEMS

Generally, all methods of tacking/basting should form a grid, often dictated by the patches in the quilt. There should not usually be a gap bigger than 6in (15cm) between the tacking/basting stitches. If the patchwork does not have a grid to follow, use your hand span as a ready guide. I find it easier to work to a grid system when tacking/basting. Since I always use the same system, I don't have to think or plan – just tack/baste! Below is the way I hand tack/baste my quilts when they are on the floor. It smooths out any wrinkles or puffs that may arise. Tools to make it quicker or more comfortable include thimbles, spoons, masking tape and a kneeling mat or knee pads.

Step One Press the backing fabric and lay it on the floor WS upwards. Pat it flat. Secure to the floor with tabs of masking tape at the corners and the mid-points on all four sides. Do NOT stretch the fabric: you'll find it will pucker, when the tacking/basting stitches are in and the masking tape comes off.

Step Two Lay the wadding/batting on top of the backing fabric. If it helps, fold the wadding/batting into four and line up the outside edge with the corner of the backing fabric then unfold a quarter at a time. Pat it flat.

Step Three Press the patchwork top for the last time, then centre it on top of the wadding/batting, RS up. Again, fold into quarters if this helps. Pat flat. Add some tabs of masking tape at the corners.

Step Four Pin the three layers together in the centre, at the corners and the mid-point on each side. This is just to keep things in place while you tack/baste.

Step Five If you are hand tacking/basting, begin with a knot and a backstitch to secure your thread. Start by tacking/basting the diagonals (**A**). If necessary, use a teaspoon to bring the needle up out of the quilt for ease, or use your thimble to protect your fingers. Finish with a backstitch. You never need to have your hand under the quilt; you are working from the top all of the time. This way you do not disturb the layers.

Step Six Tack/baste across the middle in both directions (**B**). Remove the pins as you come across them.

Step Seven Using your hand span as a guide, tack/baste in rows from the centre, working towards the outside edge (**C**). When this section is full, move round to the next (**D**). There are four sections to fill in this way, always starting from the middle and working towards the outside edge (**E** and **F**).

Step Eight When complete, tack/baste ¼in (5mm) away from the outside edge of the quilt sandwich. This will eventually be removed, and will stop the edges getting tatty or stretched before the quilt is quilted.

Step Nine Remove the masking tape, and pick up the quilt (and yourself) from the floor! If you like, you can now fold over the extra wadding/batting and backing fabric and tack/baste it abutting the edge of the quilt.

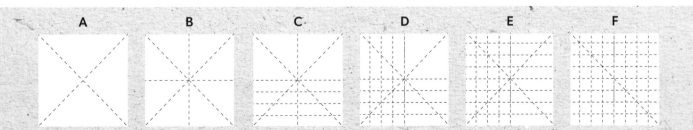

A   B   C   D   E   F

SAFETY-PIN TACKING/BASTING

For large quilts you'll need a lot of safety pins, and buying multiple packs of these can be a large outlay to start with. I'd recommend building up your safety-pin supply gradually over time. I started off just safety-pin tacking/basting small quilts, as I had a limited number of pins; as I purchased more over time I was able to use them on bigger quilts. Slowly accumulating is not only better for your pocket, it also ensures that you like that way of working. There is nothing worse than buying a huge amount of pins and then finding that the method is not for you. If you discover you enjoy this method, you will see how handy pin tacking/basting can be, as you can use the pins over and over again. Some people find the pins with pin covers easier on the hands – they give you something bigger to get hold of, and 'magically' the open pins do not stick together in clumps when stored.

Safety pins with covers.

◇ Lay out the quilt sandwich, but do not pin (see steps 1–3 on page 59). Starting from the centre of the quilt, and from the top/RS, use the safety pins to hold the layers together. Insert the pin and bring it back up through all three layers. This is where a teaspoon will ease the fingers as you bring the point of the pin up against their edge and clip the pin closed.

◇ The pins should be placed neither too closely nor too far from each other. Use your clenched fist as a gauge for pin placement – about 4in (10cm) apart.

◇ When the quilt is covered with pins, tack around the edge as described in step 8 on page 59.

REQUIREMENTS:

One table at a comfortable height. I'm using a picnic table with a smooth surface. If you are using a dining table, make sure it's protected with a thick cloth or cutting mat, so the table doesn't get marked by the pins or clamps. If the table is not high enough to work at comfortably, invest in some plastic piping that will fit on to the bottom of the legs, increasing the height. Piping can be cut easily with a hacksaw. Table risers are also good for adjusting the table height.

Chair. I use an office chair, so I can adjust the height as I tack/baste.

Masking tape

Cocktail sticks (tooth picks)

Bulldog clips or spring clamps

TABLE-TOP TACKING/BASTING

This is a great way to tack/baste a quilt when laying things out on the floor is not a practical solution. Lack of space or lack of agility might be reasons, and you want your craft to be sustainable to your body, not increasing any aches or pains: if the way you work is uncomfortable, then you will not want to do it.

Step One Measure and mark the centre of the table with a cross, and mark the halfway points on each side of the table. Then, re-mark these positions by sticking a cocktail stick/toothpick on top using masking tape. For the centre mark, stick one in place, then cut another in half, and stick down to the table. These will need to be removed before you actually tack/baste, but you need them initially to feel the centre of the table when the fabric and wadding/batting is positioned. Some people just put the sticks on the outside edge of the table, as they are easier to remove. After some practice you will see what works best for you.

Step Two Press the backing fabric and fold it into quarters, wrong sides together. Place it on the table in one quarter section – the right side of the fabric will be facing you and, once you've unfolded it, the wrong side will be uppermost.

Step Three Begin to unfold the backing fabric. Line up the edges with the points on the sides of the table so as to keep it straight.

Continued overleaf.

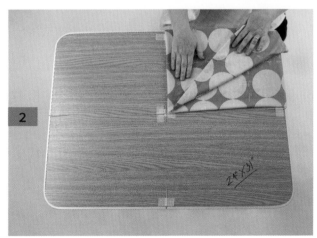

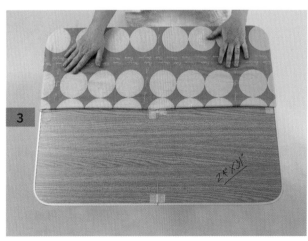

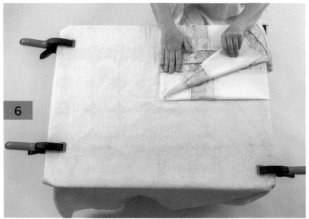

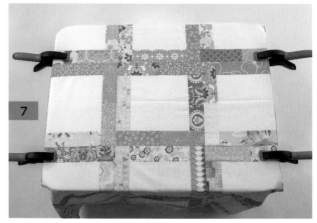

Step Four Once the backing is completely unfolded, use bulldog clips or clamps to secure the fabric to the edges of the table. If the quilt is smaller than the table, the edges that don't overhang can be taped into place. Try not to stretch the fabric – it just needs to lay flat, and this is done by gently patting the fabric and securing in place with a clamp at each corner. If the fabric is stretched, when the clamps are undone, the fabric will release and make ripples.

Step Five Now fold the wadding/batting in the same way and place on top of the backing fabric. You can feel the cocktail-stick markers through the backing fabric, so you can use these to ensure the wadding/batting is squared up and central on the backing. Smooth the wadding/batting by patting gently, without stretching it. Replace the clips already in position to hold both layers in place.

Step Six Press the quilt top and fold it into quarters, wrong side facing out. Match the centre of the top to the centre of the wadding/batting, and unfold as for the other layers. The quilt top will now be right side up.

Step Seven Pat the fabric smooth and use the clips or clamps to hold the three layers together. You can now carefully remove the cocktail sticks if you like, or wait until you need to move the quilt to tack/baste the next section.

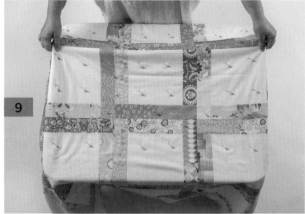

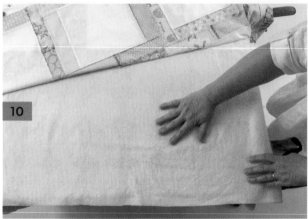

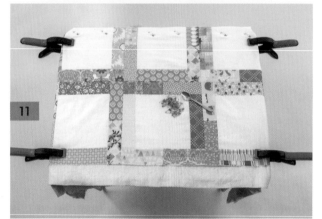

Step Eight Safety-pin tack/baste the area that is being held on the table, as detailed on page 60, or tack/baste with thread. They key to tacking/basting with thread or safety pins is to work only from the front of the quilt. If you find it hard to push the needle or the pin heads up from the table, use a teaspoon as shown.

Step Nine When the area of the quilt on top of the table is tacked/basted, take off the clips (and tape if using) and shift the layers towards or away from you so the next untacked/unbasted area is on the table top.

Step Ten Secure the side of the quilt that has been tacked/basted, then pat the backing flat and secure with clips. Make sure the wadding/batting is flat again on the backing, as shown.

Step Eleven Reposition the quilt top in place. Use tape if needed and replace the last two clamps. Tack/baste as before. Continue like this until the entire quilt is tacked/basted. You will need to move the quilt between three to nine times to completely tack/baste it. When this is complete, tack/baste ¼in (5mm) away from the outside edge all round the quilt top, as per step 8 on page 59.

Quilting

The quilting of string quilts often needs an overall approach: don't just look at each block or fabric, but choose a design that will suit a larger area and help bring the whole quilt together.

'Utility quilting designs' are frequently seen in old string quilts. These designs were seen as something that needed to be done quickly, to get the quilt onto a bed and slept under as soon as possible. These quilts were not seen as great heirlooms to be stored for special occasions, so the quilting often reflects that: the designs were quick and easy to do, and would often feature tying and thicker threads. That ethos is reflected in many of the quilts and projects in this book.

MARKING

My favourite way to mark my quilts is with a Hera marker. This is a small plastic tool of Japanese origin, which you use to indent your quilting designs onto the fabric. Bodkins embedded in a cork for ease of holding, or even your fingernail can do the same job, leaving a crease in the fabric that you can follow with your quilting stitch. This method is non-invasive and uses no inks, so there is no worry about harmful chemicals or needing to get rid of the marks afterwards. When the quilt is washed, any creases that weren't quilted over will disappear.

Alternative methods include a chalk wheel or Chaco Liner, a sliver of dried soap or soapstone pencils. With any method you use, do make sure that it will erase after it has served its purpose, and that it does not leave damaging chemical residue on your work.

STRING QUILT DESIGNS

The designs used for many string quilts are fast and simple to work, often needling little to no marking. This all contributes to the usefulness of the quilts and speed in the process.

Whether the designs are worked by hand or machine will depend on your preference of style, time and facilities.

Designs that work well for string quilts include:

◇ cross-hatch quilting

◇ diagonal-line quilting

◇ in-the-ditch quilting

◇ Amish Wave/Baptist Fan quilting

◇ elbow quilting

◇ straight-line/matchstick quilting.

Some work best on the machine, others by hand. Each method can offer its own advantages to the quilter.

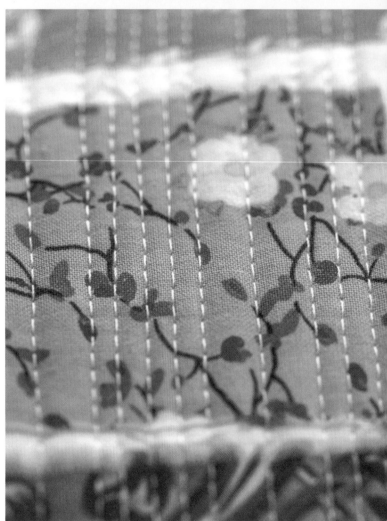

Matchstick quilting on the Tiled + Quilted Shirt-backed Pillow (see pages 150–153).

HAND QUILTING

starting the stitch

Start by cutting a length of thread as long as your arm. Tie a knot in the end you just cut. Thread the free end into the needle. You need to insert the needle down through the top layer of fabric and wadding/batting then come up where you want to start, pulling on the thread so that the knot pops through the top fabric and is embedded in the wadding/batting. The embedded thread will be quilted over, securing the thread further.

If the knot gets stuck

If the knot is stubborn, use the point of your sewing needle to poke open the weave of the fabric to expand the hole where the knot needs to go through. Gently pull the thread until the knot goes into the wadding/batting and then, using the needle again, push the threads back into place.

finishing the stitch

If the thread is running out, or you've finished your stitching, you will need to finish off securely. Make sure you leave enough thread – this will be about 5–6in (13–15cm) of thread.

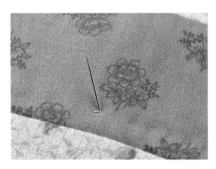

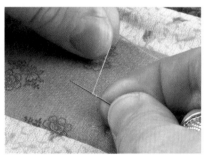

Step One Make the last stitch, going all the way through to the back of the quilt with the needle. Bring the needle up at the beginning of the stitch.

Step Two Pull the thread through and wrap it around the needle two to three times, keeping the thread close to the quilt. The number of wraps will depend on how thick the thread is, and how densely woven the fabric is too. Essentially, you are making a knot that will pull through easily.

Step Three Push the wrapped needle back through the fabric and into the wadding/batting, just underneath the middle of the last stitch, and travelling a needle's length away from the stitching. As you pull the thread a knot will form that needs to be gently pulled through to embed it in the wadding/batting. Snip the tail of thread close to the quilt top.

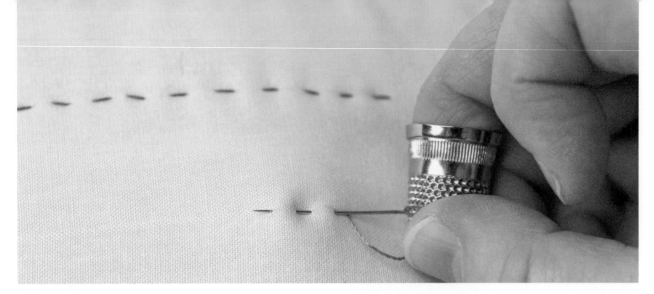

big-stitch quilting

This style of quilting uses a relatively thick thread and big stitches. The stitch length is often longer on the top surface of the quilt and smaller on the bottom. Big-stitch quilting is a bold style of quilting and the designs are usually fairly widely spaced, therefore needing fewer lines, and taking less time to quilt.

◇ Follow the sequence on starting the stitch (see opposite), and continue on. As you make the stitches, try to work with a rhythm to create even but large stitches that go through all three layers.

◇ I keep the needle hand still with the needle horizontal, moving only the finger that is on the underside of the quilt to create the stitches. Try different motions to see which is comfortable for you and creates the even stitches you want.

◇ I find it helpful to have a thimble on the middle finger of the needle hand for pushing the needle through, and a ridged thimble on the index finger of the hand under the quilt. The finger under the quilt pushes the layers up, creating a little 'hill' with the ridge of the thimble, which the needle is pushed against to make the stitch.

◇ When you have about 6in (15cm) of thread left in the needle, finish off and then start a new length of thread (see opposite).

◇ For the needle, use a size 6 Embroidery, Betweens (quilting), Chenille or Sashiko needle. For the thread, use 8wt or 12wt Coton Perle, size 167 Coton à Broder or 12wt Aurifil.

stitching in the ditch

Hand quilting with big stitches and bold thread works well for this quilting. It needs no marking as the stitches are worked in the dip of the seam of the patchwork. It has been used to good effect on the Basic String Block quilt on pages 108–111. The stitches are worked on the blue fabric with the seam pressed away from it, hence the ditch of the lower side. There is no SA to quilt through, and the stitches show up nicely too.

stitching in straight lines

These include straight parallel lines, diagonal lines at either a 45-degree or 60-degree angle, and cross-hatching and straight grids (see also page 74). Mark the lines with a ruler and a Hera marker for ease and accuracy. You can mark all the lines you intend to quilt, or leave gaps and then quilt freehand in the spaces. This approach saves time and resources.

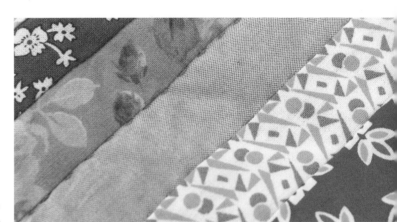

Big-stitch line quilting in the ditch along the edges of the blue strips in the Basic String Block quilt (see pages 108–111).

mennonite tacks

This stitch holds the three layers together just like regular big stitch, but with some added texture, for a bolder look. It is a cross between a stitch and knot as the little stitch acts to secure the long stitch, stopping any puckering. The stitches can be placed in conjunction with the piecing on the quilt, i.e. at seam junctions or the centre of patches, or it can be used randomly.

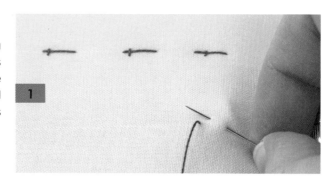

Step One Start off by embedding the knot in the wadding/batting along the line that you will be stitching along (see page 66). Don't come up right at the start of the line, as the first part of the stitch is to go backwards, and you need to allow room to do this. Insert the needle backwards (like making a backstitch), going through all the layers and coming up just before the start of the stitch and just above it.

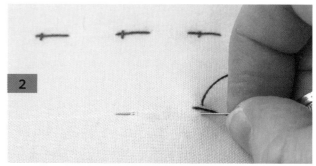

Step Two Push the needle into the first two layers just below the long stitch and let the needle travel through the wadding/batting to come up at the next stitch, about a needle's length away.

Step Three Continue on in this way and finish off the final stitch with the little stitch that crosses the long one. The spacing of the stitches can be dependent on the length of your needle, and should form a natural rhythm.

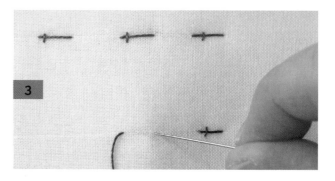

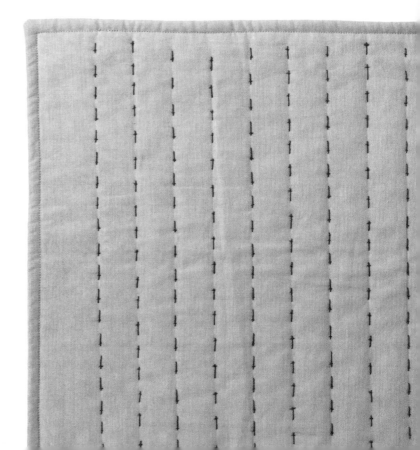

elbow quilting

Confusingly for us quilters, elbow quilting can also refer to a slightly different (but equally as useful) design for quilting string quilts – I will go into detail about this alternative version on pages 70 and 71.

The version on this page is very beginner friendly. Either divide the whole quilt into quarters, as I have done with the Wonky Squares quilt on pages 116–121, or quilt smaller areas or groups of blocks.

You can mark the design with a standard rotary-cutting ruler, but I like the ease of using a square ruler. Buy the biggest you can: a 12½in (31.75cm) square ruler is often the most useful. I use 2in (5cm) increments to mark the lines, so for a 12in (30.5cm) square block the last long line would be in the ditch of the block seam.

Step One Start with the block in the lower right-hand corner (or left-hand corner if you are left-handed). Position the square ruler in the bottom corner of the block, 2¼in (5.5cm) from the raw edge of the patchwork. This includes the ¼in (5mm) SA of the outside edge of the patchwork. Mark the two sides of the square.

Step Two Move the ruler in towards the centre of the block, using the 2in (5cm) lines to match up with the first lines drawn. Mark the lines. You may find that the 2in (5cm) lines you are marking coincide with seams in your patchwork. That is fine; you will still be quilting along these, even if you do not need to mark them.

Step Three Continue in this way until the square unit is covered. The last lines of quilting will be in the ditch around the seam of the entire unit.

Step Four Once one unit is marked, you can either move on to the next unit or quilt the one you've just marked. I like to mark then quilt each unit along the row until the bottom row is complete, then move to the next row up and repeat.

Step Five Continue in this way until the patchwork top is marked then quilted all over.

Elbow quilting a sixteen-block quilt. Note that the seams between blocks coincide with the quilt lines, and become part of the design.

amish wave

This design goes by various names thanks to the many church groups and individuals who used the design frequently. These names include elbow quilting (as noted on the previous page), Mennonite Fan, Baptist Fan and, simply, Wave. There may be different approaches to the size or the way the pattern is made, but they all have the same result. These designs need minimal marking, and generally can be quilted in one direction in an easy movement. They are a repeated pattern that can be sewn all over the quilt top, and generally do not take account of the patchwork.

Historically, they were designs quilted out of necessity: they were quick to quilt compared to elaborate feathers and wreaths, and the designs could be created from items that were common in most homes, such as cups, saucepan lids, and the length of the quilter's arm from hand to elbow for the really large waves. They were popular in quilts of the Depression era, and commonly used thicker threads to hold the layers together.

The design is quilted from the outside edge of the quilt working in towards the centre, or in rows from bottom to top. If a quilt was positioned in a square frame and being quilted by a group of people, one person could sit on each side and quilt the design, working in towards the centre of the quilt. If you quilt on a frame with rollers, you would quilt the design in rows, starting at the bottom of the quilt and working towards the top as you rolled the next part of the quilt on.

This is a popular design for a number of reasons. The fan is quilted on the bias of the fabric, which seems to give more readily under the needle and so make it easier to quilt. The design covers the quilt all over, ignoring the piecing and so acts as a unifying feature. It can be stitched by any level of quilter and so is a good choice for a beginner. It can be quilted by groups around a frame, and although the design is mainly seen with single lines of quilting it can also be worked with the lines of quilting in groups of two or three.

A template makes it easy to create even waves. You can make your own to any size you require by using either a compass or with any circular household object – see opposite. Alternatively, you can use the template on page 175.

To quilt, stitch parallel lines within each wave that gradually get smaller, using a needle or the width of a finger between each line to keep the distance consistent.

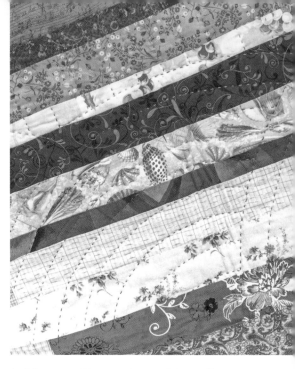

Amish wave on Housetop Sawtooth Star quilt (see pages 138–143).

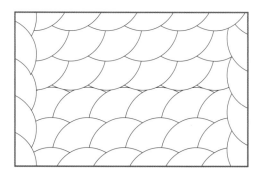

Amish Wave worked from the outside in.

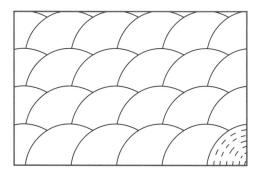

Amish Wave worked in rows from the bottom to the top. Parallel lines of stitching are then worked inside each wave.

making a wave template with a compass

Step One Set the compass to the size of the arc you would like, and place it in the corner of a sheet of paper. Draw the quarter circle.

Step Two Now move the compass point to where the circle line touched the bottom edge of the paper and draw another arc from the paper edge up to meet the first arc. This second shape is the template for the quilting design. Either trace onto template plastic or glue to card and cut out.

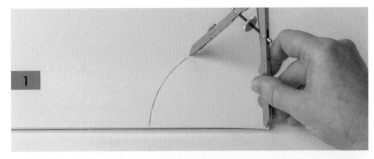

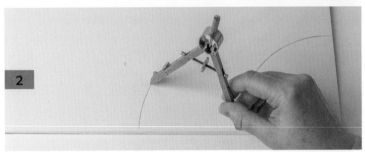

making a wave template with a plate

Step One Draw around a round object such as a plate, saucepan lid or pan onto a piece of paper. Cut out the circle and fold it into quarters, as shown.

Step Two Aligning the straight edges of the quarter circle in the bottom right-hand corner of a sheet of card or template plastic, draw around the curve to create the first arc.

Step Three Unfold the paper to make a half circle and align with the bottom and right-hand edges of the paper. Draw around this shape, from the bottom left upwards, until the line of the second arc meets the line of the first arc.

Step Four Remove the paper circle, and cut out the second shape, which is the template for your fan quilting.

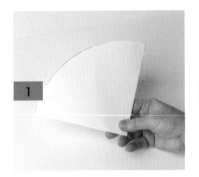

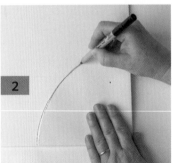

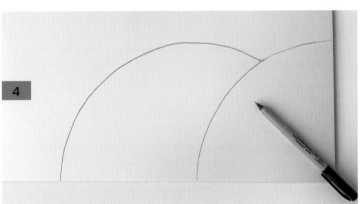

HAND TYING A QUILT

Technically this is not quilting, but it's one of the simplest ways to secure a quilt without using a sewing machine.

Tying can be done with a single thread and a simple reef knot, or more elaborately with multiple threads and more complicated knots. Experiment with different threads, thicknesses and thread-tail lengths to see which work best with your project. I most commonly use doubled thread and a reef knot.

When tying the quilt, you can start with a long thread in the needle, often twice the length of your arm. Generally, these ties or tufts will be at the seam junctions of the patches, giving an easy grid to follow. If, however, you do not have such a pattern to follow, here is a simple method to create a grid.

This vintage scrap quilt has a soft, thick wadding/batting and the layers have been tied at regular intervals with thick cotton thread.

making a grid

Take a piece of quilters' graph paper measuring 18in (45.75cm); if you don't have a piece large enough, tape sheets together to create one. With a pencil and using the lines on the paper, mark an even grid – the distance between lines can be either your hand span (about 6in or 15cm) or a your closed fist (about 4in or 10cm). When you are happy with your grid, fold the paper along the rows of marks and snip out a diamond at each point. Continue until all the marks are replaced by a hole. You can now place the paper over the quilt and, using a pencil, mark where you want to tie the quilt.

This method will also work with a piece of checked gingham cloth and will give you a larger sheet of grid to work with.

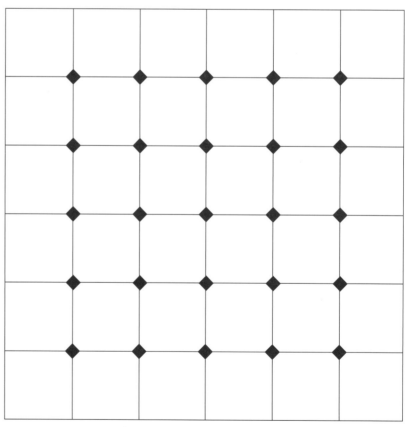

Diagram demonstrating the diamond-shaped cuts in your grid template.

Making a reef knot

Also known as a square knot, this is the most common tying knot and most of us will be familiar with it. To make one:

Step One Insert the needle through all three layers of the quilt, from the front of the quilt and coming up ¼in (5mm) away from the start. Don't pull the thread all the way through.

Step Two Re-insert the needle at the starting point, through all the layers.

Step Three Bring the needle up where you came up in step 1 and then pull the thread tightly.

Step Four Loop the left thread over the right and through the loop.

Step Five Pull tight and repeat, passing the right thread over the left and through the loop.

Step Six Pull tight and snip the excess thread to finish.

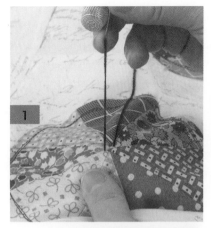

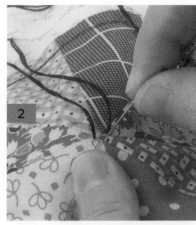

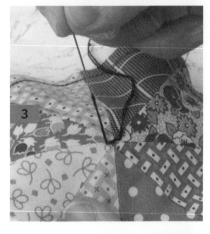

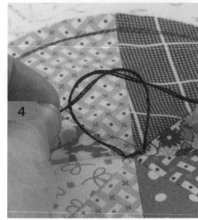

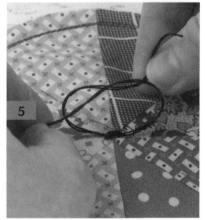

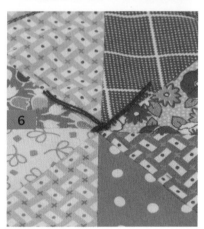

MACHINE QUILTING

Quilts can be quilted on your domestic machine or sent out for long-arm quilting. There is no shame in having a professional long-arm quilter quilt for you; it's getting it finished and closer to being used. Some of the quilts in this book were professionally quilted, often with a design you could emulate at home on your own machine if you wished. The vermicelli quilting on the Blue String Stars quilt on pages 102–107 was professionally worked, but then I added some big-stitch quilting in a contrasting thread. It is nice to work in this way – having the professional tackle what you may not feel you could have achieved on your machine, then adding your own signature to the quilting.

straight-line quilting

For this method of machine quilting, the stitch length is set by you on the machine. You may find it easier to use a walking (even-/dual-feed) foot as it helps all the layers work through at the same pace, and prevents dragging and distortion. This foot can also be used when you bind the quilt, for the same reasons.

Matchstick quilting is essentially the same as straight-line quilting, but the lines are stitched much more closely together. If you're new to it, you could mark lines over the quilt before stitching, with the help of a ruler. However, often I stitch matchstick lines using the width of my presser foot as a guide.

cross-hatch quilting

This design can be worked over the entire quilt top. Use a long ruler and a Hera marker for marking the lines, either using the patchwork/string design to help you position the lines or drawing your own lines over the patchwork. The lines should lie at either a 45-degree or 60-degree angle across the whole quilt. You can also stitch horizontal lines across the points of the diamonds to create triangles. All of these options are shown in the diagrams, right.

As with straight-line quilting, cross-hatched lines can be stitched closely together, matchstick style.

vermicelli quilting

This is an all-over, free-motion quilting design that is worked by machine over any patchwork pattern. Set up your sewing machine by lowering the feed dogs (or, if your machine is a slightly older model and doesn't have the capability to do this, by setting the stitch length to '0') and install an open-toe darning foot. The quilting pattern is 'self-guided', as you control the size of the 'swirls' and the density of stitching yourself.

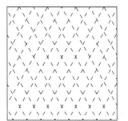

60-degree angle cross-hatching.

45-degree angle cross-hatching.

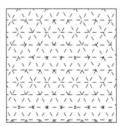

Horizontal lines added to 60-degree angle cross-hatching, creating equilateral triangles.

Vermicelli quilting.

Cross-hatched matchstick quilting on the Snowball Pincushion
(see pages 158–161).

Straight line matchstick quilting on the Snowball Pincushion.

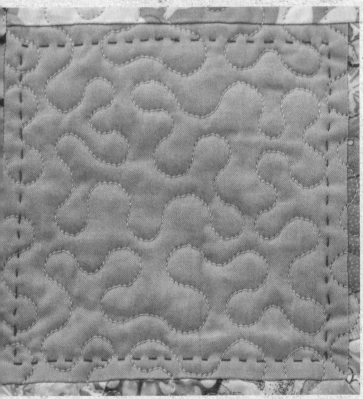

Vermicelli quilting on the Blue String Stars quilt
(see pages 102–107).

Cross-hatch quilting on the Vintage Crumb Log Cabin quilt
(see pages 90–95).

Crumb stitch experiments

And just when you thought that using up the strings from squaring up your fabrics was as far as using every piece could go, there are the crumbs!

Crumbs are the end bits that are cut off the strings. Usually, I find myself with a handful of these little pieces each time I make string blocks. They are too small to be in a string block but seem too big to discard. By sewing them together you can create a new fabric or patch, and by using them individually they can be the start of Log Cabin blocks. They can also be used in tile blocks, and Japanese boro-inspired pieces. They are also a lovely way to experiment without really risking anything as the fabric pieces were likely going to be discarded anyway.

You can call these coasters, mats or even mini quilts to frame on the wall, and they can be bound or the edges left free. Whatever you call them or do with them, I feel sure that you will be happy knowing how resourceful you have been by putting those precious pieces of fabric to good use, and from the fun you had sewing them.

1 Creating crumb fabric Collect together your crumbs, and start sewing similar-length pieces together in pairs. It's a very instinctive, organic process as you basically work with what you have at each stage of stitching. I finger-press or use a seam roller after each seam, and if something needs a little trimming I will do that. As pieces get larger, I aim to make them big enough so they can be sewn to other units. If they are of a size to be something useful, then I layer, quilt then bind. If the block or unit is still quite small, you can use it as the centre for a Log Cabin block.

2 Machine-stitch experiments The example, right, is a tile block that features overcast/serge stitch, but you could experiment with other stitches such as zigzag stitch or other decorative stitches. It is a method used frequently by the textile artist Anne Kelly to great effect. I've used the machine stitch to hold the pieces in place and quilted through the background, wadding/batting and lining at the same time.

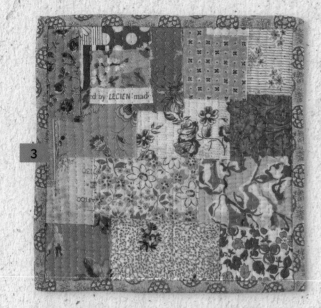

3

4a

4b

3 Hand-stitch experiments Mini quilts like this are ideal for experimenting with hand stitches. This piece was quilted with a matchstick design using big-stitch quilting, in the style of Japanese boro. Derived from the Japanese 'boroboro', meaning something tattered or repaired, boro refers to the practice of reworking and repairing textiles (often clothes or bedding) through piecing, patching and stitching. Fabric pieces – in this case, the crumbs – are overlapped on a base cloth (or in this case, the wadding/batting and backing). The pieces are then kept in place with hand stitches.

4 Tile blocks These types of crumb blocks (sometimes known as stone-wall or pavement quilts) have a long and interesting history in patchwork. They can be seen in English quilts as far back as the early 1800s, and the style is seen in US quilts after this date too. Basically, odd-sized scraps and crumbs are appliquéd onto a background, leaving a narrow space of the background fabric between the pieces. Triangles and other geometric shapes are common, but occasionally you can see more free-form shapes too. The result looks like a tiled floor with grouting between the appliquéd pieces. The shapes are hand appliquéd to the background and then the piece is layered and quilted before binding. Usually the SAs of the shapes are turned under as they're appliquéd (see **4a**); however, there are versions where the fabric is left with fraying edges, and running stitch or backstitch is sewn around the shape, inside the raw edge, to secure it to the background (see **4b**). Sample **4a** has been hand quilted with big-stitch around each shape; sample **4b** has been quilted with big-stitch to make a matchstick pattern.

Binding

Once the layers of the quilt are quilted, it can be prepared for binding. If you use the bagging-out technique (see pages 82 and 83), essentially you will 'bind' the quilt before quilting it. But in most cases a binding will be added or the backing fabric turned over to the front of the quilt after quilting.

MAKING BINDING TAPE

You can use one fabric or a number of fabrics in one binding. The easiest way to use at least four different fabrics in a binding is to sew the Square-cornered Binding on page 84, using one fabric for each side of the quilt.

The binding for my quilts is most often made from strips cut across the width of the fabric. Cutting strips from the width of fabric is an economical way to cut the binding and gives it a strong straight edge. The strips of fabric will be folded over to make what is known as a 'double binding', which is very durable and gives a nice clean edge to your quilt.

The sample in the steps is hand stitched, but you can sew by machine if you have it to hand.

joining strips for binding

The strips of fabric will need to be joined to make a continuous length. I use a bias or crossway join here to eliminate bulky areas when the binding is sewn and folded over the edge of the quilt. Use the following method, cutting 2½in (6.5cm) strips.

Step One Take one of the strips and lay another over the top, right sides together and at a 90-degree angle. Allow an extra ⅜in (1cm) of fabric along each short edge, as shown. Pin across the diagonal – you can mark in a stitch line with pencil or Hera marker, if you'd like a guide line, but with practice you can stitch it by eye.

Step Two On the far-right end (or far-left end, if you are left-handed), make a backstitch, leaving the waste knot and tail visible on the WS facing you. Stitch small running stitches across the diagonal, making a backstitch about halfway along to anchor your running stitches. At the end, make a final backstitch then knot off. Cut off the excess fabric, leaving a ¼in (5mm) seam allowance. Repeat steps 1 and 2 to join together the remaining strips.

Step Three To finish your tape, open out the tape then press the seams open. I tend not to trim off the 'ears' of the seam allowances where the strips have been joined, as these will be hidden in the binding later. You can now press your tape in half, long edges and WS together.

CONTINUOUS MITRED BINDING

This is a traditional way to bind a quilt, leaving it with a narrow binding approximately ⅜in (1cm) wide. If you bind your quilt this way, trim the backing and wadding/batting in line with the patchwork top on the front of the quilt, or you can leave the excess and trim it off after step 5.

Step One To start, prepare the mock bias join at one end of your binding as follows. Fold over one end of the strip by 90 degrees.

Step Two Trim off the excess fabric at the end of the strip, leaving a ¼in (5mm) seam allowance.

Step Three Pin the binding to the quilt top, about one-third of the way along one edge and raw edges aligned. Start with the end with the mock bias join. Sew the binding along the edge with a ¼in (5mm) seam allowance then stop ¼in (5mm) from the first corner you meet. Fold the binding at a 90-degree angle, away from the quilt and so the free long edge of the binding aligns with the next, unbound edge of the quilt.

Step Four Fold the binding back down along the next unbound edge, aligning the raw edges and creating a fold at the corner. Start sewing from the folded edge. Sew down to the next corner, and repeat to sew the rest of the binding to the quilt top.

Step Five When you have stitched all the way around the quilt, trim the binding at an angle and so it overlaps the starting (mock bias join) end by about ⅜in (1cm). Tuck the trimmed end inside the end with the mock bias join. Then, continue to stitch along the binding as before to secure the ends to the quilt top.

Step Six Trim the excess wadding/batting (if you haven't already) then turn the binding over to the back of the quilt. The corners should 'magically' mitre. Pin the binding, so the folded edge covers your stitching, then slip stitch in place along the fold. You will need to stitch the mitred corners closed, to stop them from opening.

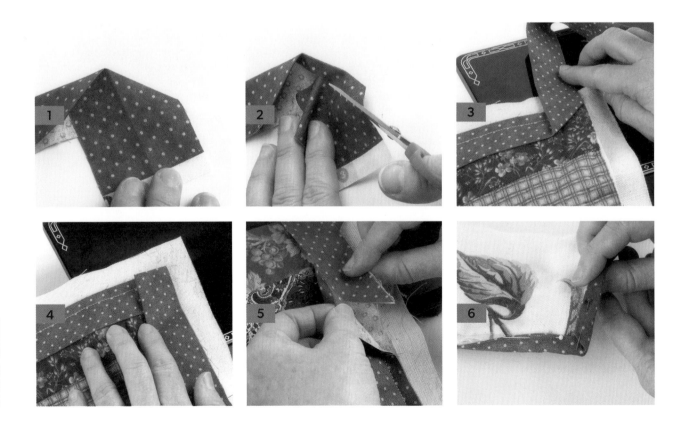

SELF-BOUND BINDING

This is a lovely method to stitch by hand, and no extra fabric is needed as you use the surplus backing fabric around the edge of your quilt to create binding. You may want to consider which fabric you choose for the backing if you are using this method, as it will show on the front of the quilt.

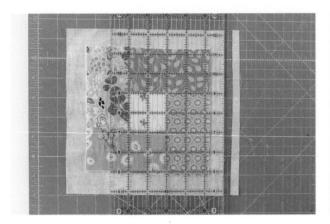

Step One After quilting, trim the wadding/batting to the size of the quilt top, then trim the backing fabric so it is ¾in (2cm) larger all round than both the quilt top and wadding/batting.

Step Two Starting in the middle of a straight side, turn the backing over so the raw edge touches the raw edge of the trimmed quilt. Fold over the backing once more, so that it covers the raw edge of the quilt top.

Step Three Repeat with the rest of the backing, round the whole quilt top. The corners should 'step', overlapping the previously folded edge as shown. Pin in place as you work.

Step Four Slip stitch the folded backing to the quilt top, along the fold. The stitches should not go through to the back of the quilt, but will be worked through the quilt top and wadding/batting. Start in the middle of a straight edge, coming up through the wadding/batting to hide the waste knot and tail behind the backing/binding. At the corners, stitch down each end/corner completely to secure it.

TURN-THROUGH OR BAGGED-OUT BINDING

With this method, the quilt is, in effect, bound before it is quilted. Use it on your quilts when you don't want binding, want a clean crisp edge to the quilt, or there is just not fabric enough to add a binding. This technique has been popular on the kantha quilts of India and is widely used in the 'North Country Quilts' in the UK, around the Durham area.

Here, I have made a coaster to demonstrate the technique, which is made up of three layers of fabric: the top, backing and an interlining. In the example here, the backing and the wadding/batting are the same size as the top fabric. The coaster is not too large, and there is very little room for movement of the fabric layers when pinned together. If you are making a quilt, you will want to allow a margin of a few inches on all sides. I add 5in (13cm) to the overall measurement of the quilt to make the backing and wadding/batting larger. Once the layers are stitched together, as shown here, the backing can be trimmed to the same size as the front of the quilt, and the wadding/batting trimmed closer to the stitching line to reduce the bulk.

Step One Smooth out the wadding/batting on a flat surface. Place the quilt backing on top of the wadding/batting, RS up, and pat flat. If you like, you can use 505 spray adhesive or safety pins here, but usually the cotton quilt back will adhere to the wadding/batting of its own accord. Centre the quilt top on top, RS down. Pin the three layers together all the way round the edge, with the pins perpendicular to the edge. Leave a gap in the middle of one side of about 3–6in (7.5–15cm), depending on the size of your project, in order to turn the quilt RS out.

Step Two Stitch around the edge of the quilt top using a ¼in (5mm) SA, removing pins as you reach them. As you come to each corner, stitch two or three stitches across it at an angle – this will create a neater corner when you turn the quilt through. Secure the stitches where you start and stop, remembering to leave your turning gap. Snip across the corners through all three layers. Using a pair of small sharp scissors, trim the wadding/batting close to the sewing line. Depending on the bulk of the wadding/batting, you may not need to do this.

Step Three Turn the quilt RS out through the turning gap; pull the corner furthest from the gap through first to allow for a smooth turn through.

Step Four Use a pair of scissors, a chopstick or a knitting needle to poke out the corners carefully.

Step Five 'Roll' the seam between your thumbs and forefingers to help it lie flat.

Step Six Either pin or use clips to keep the edge flat temporarily. To secure the flattened seam permanently, use big-stitch quilting or Mennonite tacks (see page 68). Sew along the outside edge of the quilt, just along where the bulk of the SA ends. You can now secure the three layers together if you need to, using safety pins or hand tacking/basting, ready for quilting.

SQUARE-CORNERED BINDING

This is a simple basic binding to use when you want to add some colour and strength to the edge of your quilt. This version is sewn on the machine and finished by hand. Begin by cutting strips of binding 2½in (6.5cm) wide and join them with a crossways join, so that you have four strips about 2in (5cm) longer than each side of the quilt (see page 79). Press them in half lengthways, wrong sides together.

Step One Sew one strip to the RS of the quilt, matching the raw edges and using the width of the presser foot as your seam allowance. When you reach the end, trim the binding to line up with the top fabric, if necessary. Repeat this process on the opposite side of the quilt. (An alternative is to work your way round the quilt, applying the binding Log-Cabin style.)

Step Two Trim off the surplus backing and wadding/batting in line with the raw edge of the binding. Finger press the binding away from the quilt top.

Step Three Repeat on the remaining sides of the quilt, aligning the raw edges of each strip with the raw edges of the binding strips already attached and pressed open.

Step Four At the corners, trim away the surplus fabric and wadding/batting to make turning the binding in easier.

Step Five Fold the binding over onto the back of the quilt and pin it in place. Fold the corners so that the raw edges are concealed. Slip stitch the folded edge down, sewing along the open edges at the corners.

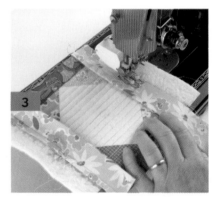
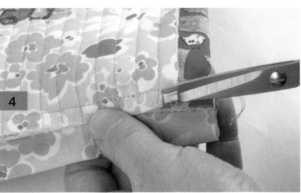

HACKED MITRED CORNERS WITH A SQUARE-CORNER FINISH

Since seeing an antique quilt with a binding consisting of three mitred corners and one square corner, this is now my go-to method for finishing my quilts, and this is what I've used on the crumb quilts on pages 76 and 77. There is no worry about neatly joining the ends of binding together, as seen in the 'Continuous mitred binding' method on page 80, and at a glance the casual observer won't notice one of the corners doesn't look like the rest.

Step One Start as you would for square-cornered binding, with one binding end lined up along one edge on the front of the quilt, raw edges matching, and from one corner.

Step Two At the next three corners, fold and stitch as you would for a mitred corner (see page 80).

Step Three As you approach the last corner, fold the stitched binding along the next edge away from the quilt, as shown.

Step Four Lay the rest of the binding along the edge, then stitch right to the edge. Trim off the excess binding.

Step Five On the back of the quilt and at the square corner, trim away the surplus fabric (and wadding/batting, if necessary) to make the corner less bulky.

Step Six Turn the binding to the back of the quilt, and cover the raw edges and stitch line of the binding worked from the front of the quilt. Fold and pin the mitred corners as per step 6 on page 80; for the square corner, fold and pin as shown, so the corners are 'stepped'. Then slip stitch in place along the fold.

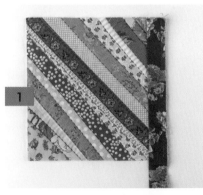

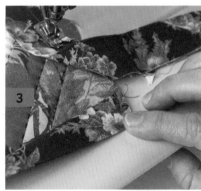

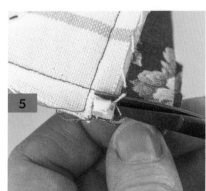

labelling + aftercare

LAUNDERING QUILTS

Once your quilt is finished, it may need laundering. This will freshen the quilt after so much handling and remove any markings and residue from the quilting process. Also, depending on the wadding/batting used, laundering will shrink the quilt a little and emphasize the quilting stitches.

Quilts are quite sturdy and can easily be washed in a washing machine. Only antique and fragile quilts are best washed by hand. I put my quilts in the machine on a gentle cycle at 30°C (86°F) with detergent specially formulated for colours. If you pre-wash fabrics and have used reclaimed garments for the quilt there should not be an issue with colour bleeding. If you are concerned about colour bleeding, put in a few 'colour catchers'.

Most of the time, I will only wash my quilts when I can dry them outside, especially on a windy day. This is an obvious way to save resources, and avoid needing to tumble dry. If I cannot do that then I will put the quilt in the tumble dryer long enough to take out the excess water, then I'll put the quilt in the airing cupboard or over a clothes airer to finish off. Once the quilt is dry it can be used, and will not need ironing.

LABELLING YOUR QUILT

Once your quilt is sewn and bound, it's worth giving a thought to labelling it. If we think about how many lovely vintage and antique quilts that there are to inspire us, then look to see who made them, many are anonymous. It is a shame to think of all that work, and yet there is no acknowledgement of the maker.

The label can just be your name and the date. If the quilt is a gift, perhaps include a short message and the recipient's name too.

re-using fabrics

It is worth thinking about using discarded vintage embroidered coasters or doilies as fabric for labels (see the photographed examples below). These can often be bought cheaply in charity/thrift/op shops. Choose designs to which you can add your name and the date at the very least. Wash and press them first. To stabilize them to write on, iron them to the shiny side of some freezer paper (see page 41). Once written on they can be peeled away, and the paper reused next time.

handwritten

The labelling can be written directly on to the back of the quilt with a permanent marker pen, or on to a muslin/calico label that is then stitched to the quilt.

pre-printed labels

Many craft shops sell fabrics consisting of decorative blank labels. Buy these by the yard or metre to cut out and use on your projects. Labels can also be ordered from name-tape suppliers, and you can customize these with various motifs and phrases. If you find that you have labels that were cut out of school uniforms over the years and saved, you can use these as part of the labelling process.

embroidered + cross-stitched labels

Many talented quilters embroider too. Consider embellishing your written label with simple stitching such as backstitch. With a little planning and some graph paper, you can work a cross-stitch label. A special canvas, known as waste canvas, can be used on top of the muslin/calico and the threads pulled away afterwards to leave your stitching on the muslin/calico.

printed computer labels

If writing your label is proving a little daunting, then you can produce one on the computer instead. Simply create your label as a document and then print it out on to special fabric sheets. Just follow the instructions to make the printing permanent, and stitch the label to the quilt.

THE PROJECTS
Quilts
—

Vintage Crumb Log Cabin

Quilt size: 72½ x 76½in (184.25 x 194.25cm)

This quilt was inspired by the blocks in a string quilt from the late 1800s. There were lots of blocks cut to the same size, but each was made from scraps and strings. Some of the blocks had a random Log Cabin design, so I focused on this element.

After making the blocks (see pages 35–38) and when I started to square them up for the quilt top, it transpired that I had blocks that fell into two sizes – 7in (17.75cm) square and 8in (20.25cm) square finished. However, I figured out I could use them together: by arranging eight 7in (17.75cm) square blocks in a row and seven 8in (20.25cm) square blocks in another row, it ensured each row – regardless of the blocks used – measured 56in (approx. 142cm) in length. I had enough blocks for eight rows in total, and so my quilt design came together. This approach to creating patchwork quilts can be called 'improvisational' or 'organic', but for me it was making do with what I had and what I had time to stitch. These are constraints that people making scrap and string quilts in the past would have known about and worked with too.

The vintage quilt that inspired this one had a border comprised of four- and nine-patch blocks, so I decided to extend this idea by making the border for my own quilt four squares deep. I had a lot of spare pre-cut strips in various sizes, measuring 10in (25.5cm), 5in (12.75cm) and 2½in (6.5cm) long, and creating a deep border made it possible to use up as many of these as I could.

If you are a fan of using a thread saver on your machine (see page 17), consider substituting it with a pair of 2½in (6.5cm) squares instead. Often called 'leaders and enders' (a method of scrap sewing pioneered by Bonnie K. Hunter), this method means that you are sewing two patches together when you would usually use a thread saver. The joined pair can later be used to make a bigger patchwork piece. In this case, the border for this quilt.

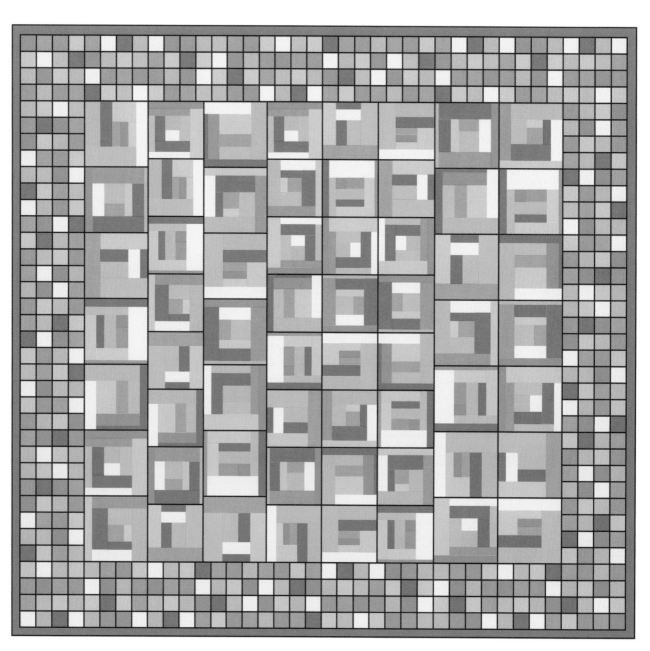

Vintage Crumb Log Cabin quilt design.

MEASUREMENTS

Quilt size:
72½ x 76½in (184.25 x 194.25cm)

Finished block sizes:
7in (17.75cm) square and
8in (20.25cm) square

REQUIREMENTS

Blocks:
Scraps, crumbs and strips and strings
from your scrap basket

Border:
Thirty-four strips, 2½in (6.5cm) x WoF

OR one hundred and thirty-two
5in (12.75cm) squares

OR thirty-four 10in (25.5cm) squares

Wadding/batting:
82 x 94in (208.25 x 238.75cm)

Backing:
188in (477.5cm) x WoF

Binding:
20in (51cm) x WoF

Notions:
Square rotary-cutting ruler – 12½in (31.75cm)
is the most useful size

FABRIC CUTTING

Blocks:
Sixty squares or rectangles for the starting
centre piece

Border:
Depending on your approach to sewing:

cut five hundred and twenty-eight 2½in (6.5cm)
squares to chain piece into pairs

OR leave the strips as is and use the string-fabric
method (see page 35). This will mean you will have a
less random look as many fabric combinations will be
repeated

OR if using 10in (25.5cm) and 5in (12.75cm) squares,
cut them into 2½in (6.5cm) wide strips then use the
string-fabric method (see page 35). You will have a
more random arrangement of squares, but it will be
quicker than chain piecing individual squares

Backing:
Cut into two equal lengths, remove the selvedge(s)
and join along those edges. Press the seam open.

Binding:
Cut eight 2½in (6.5cm) x WoF strips. Join with bias
joins to make a continuous length, then trim the SA to
¼in (5mm). Press the seams open. Press in half along
the length, WS together.

METHOD

Step One See pages 36–38 for making Log Cabin blocks. Make twenty-eight 8in (20.25cm) square blocks and thirty-two 7in (17.75cm) blocks.

Step Two I arranged my blocks into four rows of seven 8in (20.25cm) blocks and four rows of eight 7in (17.75cm) blocks. Join the blocks in each row RS together then press the seams open.

Step Three Arrange the rows for the patchwork top; mine went as follows, from the top down: 8in (20.25cm), 7in (17.75cm), 8in (20.25cm), 7in (17.75cm), 7in (17.75cm), 7in (17.75cm), 8in (20.25cm), 8in (20.25cm). Stitch the rows RS together then press the seams in one direction.

Step Four To make the border, you need to start off with one hundred and thirty-two pieced strips, each consisting of a row of four squares. Choose from (or combine some or all of) the approaches below, depending on your scraps. Mix up the fabric combinations as you work. You can chain piece here and snip apart when finished. Leave all seams unpressed until the rows are sewn together.

Chain piecing 2½in (6.5cm) squares (4a). Pair up and stitch the squares RS together, along one edge. Make two hundred and sixty-four pairs in total. Snip apart the chain-piecing threads between pairs. Open out the pairs then stitch them RS together to make a row of four. Repeat to make one hundred and thirty-two pieced strips of four squares. Proceed to steps 5 and 6.

Sew then cut long strips (4b). Pair up 2½in (6.5cm) wide strips and, using a smaller than usual machine stitch, sew the paired strips RS together along one long edge. Make seventeen pairs in total. Open out the strips then cut through the length every 2½in (6.5cm). Repeat to make one hundred and thirty-two pieced strips of four squares. Proceed on to steps 5 and 6.

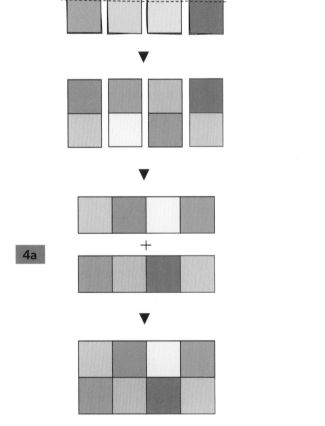

4a

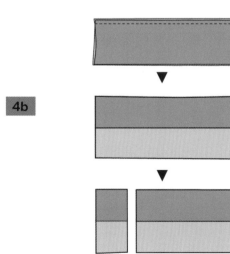

4b

5in (12.75cm) squares (4c). Sew two squares RS together, along two opposite edges. Cut in half vertically through the centre, parallel to the stitched sides, to make two 2½in (6.5cm) wide paired strips. Rotate the ruler then sub-cut each paired strip in half through the centre along the horizontal, cutting through the seams, to make four 2½in (6.5cm) paired squares. Make two hundred and sixty-four pairs in total. Open out the pairs then stitch them RS together to make a row of four. Repeat to make one hundred and thirty-two pieced strips of four squares. Proceed to steps 5 and 6.

10in (25.5cm) squares (4d). Sew two squares RS together, along two opposite edges. Cut in half vertically through the centre, parallel to the stitched sides, then sew along the open long edges of each pair RS together. Sub-cut each pair in half along the vertical again to make four 2½in (6.5cm) wide paired strips. Open out the pairs then stitch them RS together to make a column of four strips. Cut through the length every 2½in (6.5cm). Repeat to make one hundred and thirty-two pieced strips of four squares. Proceed to steps 5 and 6.

Step Five For the two short borders that are 56in (142.25cm) in length, stitch twenty-eight pieced strips RS together, mixing up the colours and alternating the direction of the SA so they knit together neatly. Press the seams in the direction they are sewn, and the long seam open. Stitch to the short sides of the patchwork top. Press the seams towards the border.

Step Six Using the same method as in the previous step, stitch the two long borders, each made using thirty-eight pieced strips. Stitch to the longest edges of the patchwork top. Press the seams towards the border.

Step Seven Layer and tack/baste the quilt with backing and wadding/batting, ready to quilt.

Step Eight This quilt was machine quilted in a cross-hatch design, with the quilt lines 1in (2.5cm) apart. However, you could machine-stitch a wider grid or hand quilt using big-stitch quilting or Mennonite tacks (see page 68). Once quilted, remove the tacking/basting stitches.

Step Nine Trim the backing and wadding/batting in line with the quilt top. Bind the quilt with your chosen method (see pages 78–85), then finish with a label if you wish (see pages 86 and 87).

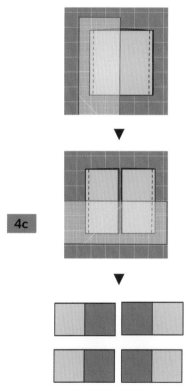

4c

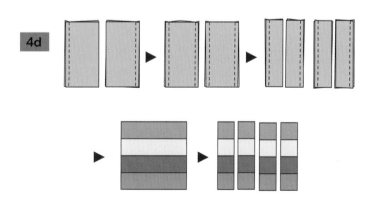

4d

String Snowball

Quilt size: 74½ x 74½in (189.25 x 189.25cm)

I've always found the Snowball pattern and all its many variations fascinating and fun to sew. But I was surprised to find so many versions of the pattern made with string-pieced blocks. I've also come across several Snowball quilts with a vivid orange or yellow background (see the bottom-right photograph on page 9 and the top-right photograph on page 11).

For my own quilt, I have gone for something a little calmer here by using a cream print for my 'snowballs'. As is often the case, I realized I wanted to make the quilt bigger and would not have enough fabric, so I've used a slightly darker cream alongside the first. This meant I could get on and sew without having to go shopping, and it means I used up more of my stash. It does also mean when I am shopping for new fabrics, I know there is a gap to be filled!

Machine quilted by Chris Farrance.

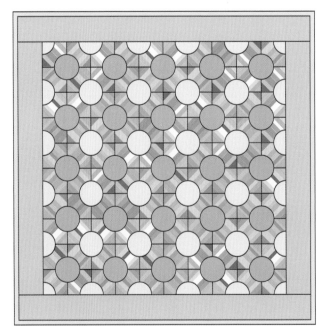

String Snowball quilt design.

MEASUREMENTS

Quilt size:
74½ x 74½in (189.25 x 189.25cm)

Finished block size:
6in (15.25cm) square

REQUIREMENTS

Blocks:
Strings from your scrap bag

Foundation – 130in (330.25cm) x WoF of sew-in light-weight interfacing

Cream circles:
I used two fabrics here as I did not have enough of either for the whole quilt. This meant creating the snowballs in two colours, which is a fun element of the quilt's design, but you can use as many as you like and have fun picking their placement.
Fabric A – 35in (90cm) x WoF
Fabric B – 35in (90cm) x WoF

Border:
52½in (135cm) x WoF – a multicoloured floral fabric works to combine all the different fabrics in the string blocks. I chose it after the blocks were made to pull things together visually.

Wadding/batting:
84in (213.5cm) square

Backing:
170in (432cm) x WoF

Binding:
20in (51cm) x WoF

Notions:
6½in (16.5cm) square rotary-cutting ruler

Templates A and B (see page 170)

FABRIC CUTTING

Blocks:
Cut twenty 6½in (16.5cm) x WoF strips of sew-in light-weight interfacing, then sub-cut them into one hundred 6½in (16.5cm) squares.

Cream circles:
Start with Fabric A. Cut ten 3½in (9cm) x WoF strips. Sub-cut them into one hundred 3½in (9cm) squares. Then, using template B, cut one hundred pieces.

Repeat the process above with Fabric B.

<u>Note:</u> you need a total of two hundred snowball pieces, so if you are using more than two fabrics, make sure you make two hundred template B shapes in total.

Border:
Cut seven 7½in (19cm) x WoF strips. Remove the selvedge then join to make a continuous length. Press the seams open.

Cut two 60½ x 7½in (153.75 x 19cm) strips.

Cut two 74½ x 7½in (189.25 x 19cm) strips.

Backing:
Cut into two equal lengths, remove the selvedge(s) and join along those edges. Press the seam open.

Binding:
Cut eight 2½in (6.5cm) x WoF strips. Join with bias joins to make a continuous length, then trim the SA to ¼in (5mm). Press the seams open. Press in half along the length, WS together.

METHOD

Step One Make one-hundred basic string blocks, referring to pages 29–31 if needed.

Step Two Use template A to draw quarter-circle curves on the back of the blocks, one in one corner and one in the opposite corner. Make sure the circles are placed perpendicular to the direction of the strips in your string block. Cut out the quarter circles. You can use these cut-out pieces in other projects, like the Snowball Pincushion on pages 158–161.

Step Three Using pins and on one block, pin one Fabric A quarter circle to a cut-out corner, RS together. Pin the middle then the outside edges first. Now add pins between these. This method of pinning ensures an even distribution around the curve. If you're pinning for hand sewing, pin on the sewing line and into the SA. If you're pinning to machine stitch, pin from the raw edge into the bulk of the block. This way the pins are easier to take out as you stitch if you are right-handed; do the opposite if you're left-handed. Repeat on the opposite cut-out corner with a Fabric B quarter circle.

Step Four Sew the Fabric A and Fabric B quarter circles in place. Open out and press.

Step Five Repeat steps 3 and 4 above with the remaining cream quarter circles and blocks, making one hundred blocks in total.

Step Six Stitch the blocks RS together in rows of ten. Pin at the seam junctions to ensure accuracy. Press the seams open. Note the direction of the pieces in each row: I've paired up the same-coloured creams in the first row. When you put the second row together pay attention to the creams and to the direction of the block, so that you are forming a lattice pattern as shown.

Continued overleaf.

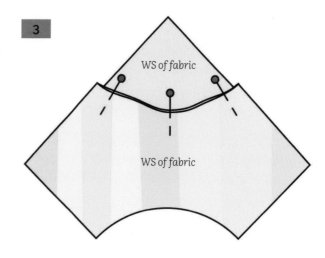

WS of fabric

WS of fabric

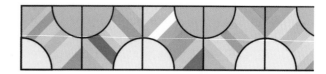

Step Seven Stitch the rows together, alternating them as detailed in the previous step and pinning at the seam junctions for accuracy. Press the seams open.

Step Eight Stitch the shorter border pieces to the sides of the patchwork. Press the seams towards the outer edges.

Step Nine Stitch the remaining long borders to the top and bottom. Press the seams towards the outer edges.

Step Ten Layer the quilt: place the backing RS down, centre the wadding/batting over the top, then centre the quilt top over these, RS up. Tack/baste the layers together, ready to quilt.

Step Eleven The quilt was quilted on a long-arm machine with a vermicelli design (see page 74); you could do something similar on your domestic machine. However, as an alternative, the quilt could easily be hand quilted around the circles and tied at the junction of the blocks.

Step Twelve Once quilted, remove any remaining tacking/ basting stitches. Trim the backing and wadding/batting in line with the quilt top. Bind the quilt with your chosen method (see pages 78–85), then finish with a label if you wish (see pages 86 and 87).

Blue String Stars

Quilt size: 77½ x 77½in (197 x 197cm)

This Eight-point Star block with set-in piecing is another scrap-busting block that quilters of the past chose to use their left-over fabrics for.

The blue stars started as a way to use some strings in my stash. But as I worked and wanted to make more blocks, I ended up cutting more strips and strings from fabrics in my stash. The background fabric for the blocks were old shirts that belonged to my husband that had seen better days. It is fun to have them live a second life in this quilt. The bold border and sashing fabric adds a nice contrast, and is a great example of a fabric pulling a string quilt together.

Machine quilted by Chris Farrance. Hand quilted by Carolyn Forster.

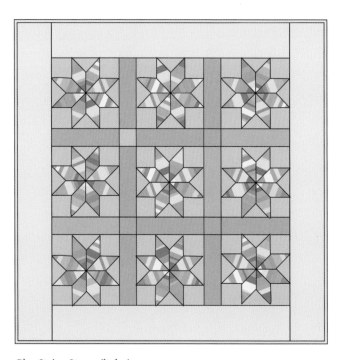

Blue String Star quilt design.

MEASUREMENTS

Quilt size:
77½ x 77½in (197 x 197cm)

Finished block size:
18in (45.75cm) square

REQUIREMENTS

Blocks:
About nine to ten string-pieced fabric panels (see page 35), each approx. 20 x 22in (50.75 x 56cm)

OR use a fabric printed with stripes

Background:
63in (160cm) x WoF

Sashing:
37in (94cm) x WoF

Posts/cornerstones:
4in (10cm) x WoF

Border:
60in (152.5cm) x WoF

Wadding/batting:
87in (221cm) square

Backing:
174in (442cm) x WoF

Binding:
20in (55cm) x WoF

Notions:
Diamond, Triangle and Square templates (see pages 172–174)

FABRIC CUTTING

Blocks:
Cut seventy-two diamonds from your string fabric or stripy fabric, using the diamond template (see the technique on page 41)

Background:
Squares: cut thirty-six 6in (15.25cm) squares.

Triangles: cut nine 9in (23cm) squares then sub-cut each along both diagonals to make thirty-six Quarter Square Triangles.

Sashing:
Cut twelve 4 x 18½in (10 x 47cm) strips.

Posts/cornerstones:
Cut four 4in (10cm) squares.

Border:
Cut seven 8½in (21.75cm) x WoF strips. Remove the selvedge(s) then join the strips to make a continuous length. Press the seams open.

Cut two 8½in x 61½in (21.75 x 156.25cm) strips.

Cut two 8½in x 77½in (21.75 x 197cm) strips.

Backing:
Cut into two equal lengths. Remove the selvedge(s), then join them RS together along one long edge. Press the seam open.

Binding:
Cut eight 2½in (6.5cm) x WoF strips. Join with bias joins to make a continuous length, then trim the SA to ¼in (5mm). Press the seams open. Press in half along the length, WS together.

METHOD

Step One To make one block, take eight diamonds. Sew the diamonds RS together in pairs, starting at the thin end and stopping ¼in (5mm) before you reach the end of the seam. Press the seam open.

Step Two Sew two pairs of diamonds RS together, again starting at the thin end and stopping ¼in (5mm) before you reach the end of the seam, as shown. Press the seam open. Repeat to make another half section.

Step Three With RS together, match up the centres of the two halves of the star and pin. Start sewing ¼in (5mm) from one end, across the centre of the star and then finish ¼in (5mm) before the end of the seam. Press the seam open.

Step Four Now set in the background. Start with one triangle. With RS together, align the two matching angles of the triangle and the diamond.

Step Five Working so the WS of the star is facing you, sew from the point of the diamond and triangle towards the 'corner' you need to sew round. When you reach the corner, stop in the centre of one seam. Leave the needle IN the work.

Step Six Lift the presser foot and pivot the fabric around so you will be stitching up the edge of the next diamond. Align the remaining short edge of the triangle and the edge of the next diamond, RS together. Sew all the way along the edge. Press the last seam towards the triangle.

Continued overleaf.

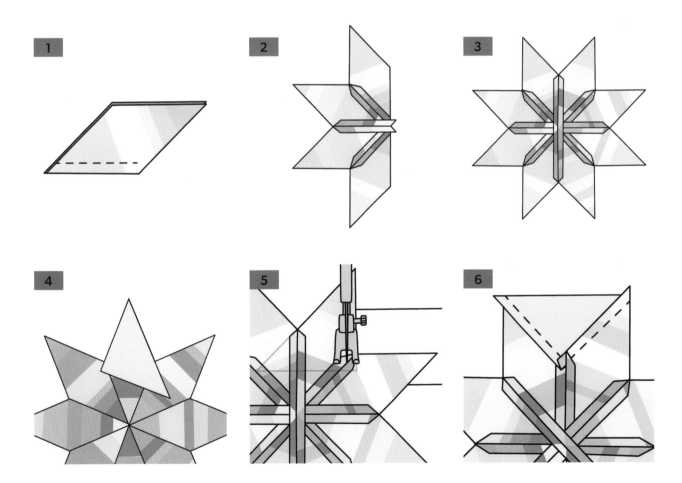

7

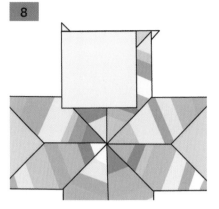

8

9

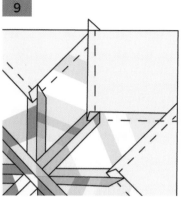

Step Seven Repeat to add three more triangles to the star unit.

Step Eight Now stitch all of the squares in place following the same method. The squares will match the new angles created and align to the raw edges.

Step Nine Once stitched, press the last seam towards the square.

STRING QUILTS

Step Ten Make nine Eight-point Star blocks overall, following the previous steps.

Step Eleven Now make the sashing rows. Stitch the sashing and posts together as shown in the illustration. Make two. Press the seams towards the sashing.

Step Twelve Make three rows with the blocks and remaining sashing strips, as shown in the illustration. Press the seams towards the sashing.

Step Thirteen Stitch the sashing and block rows RS together, as shown in the illustration. Press the seams towards the sashing rows.

Step Fourteen Stitch the short borders to the top and bottom ends of the quilt. Press the seams towards the borders.

Step Fifteen Stitch the long borders to the remaining edges of the quilt. Press the seams towards the borders.

Step Sixteen Layer the quilt: place the backing RS down, centre the wadding/batting over the top, then centre the quilt top over these, RS up. Tack/baste the layers together, ready to quilt.

Step Seventeen This was quilted in an all-over vermicelli pattern on the machine (see page 74), but would look good quilted by hand in the Amish Wave design (see pages 70 and 71). I then outlined the inner edges of the background triangles and squares with big-stitch quilting.

Step Eighteen Once quilted, remove the tacking/basting stitches then trim the edges and square up. Bind the quilt with your chosen method (see pages 78–85), then finish with a label if you wish (see pages 86 and 87).

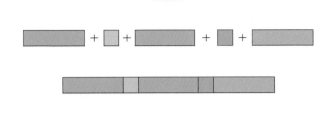

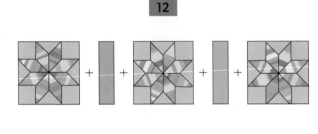

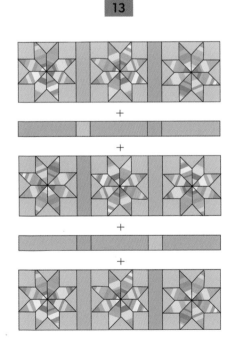

Basic String Block

Quilt size: 72½ x 72½in (184.25 x 184.25cm)

The blue strips and shirt off-cuts from the Blue String Stars quilt (see the previous pages) came into their own here: I used them for the centre strips in each block, which unifies them (see 'Focus colours' on page 49). The inspiration came from a vintage block in my collection, which has a blue-green strip along the centre of each unit for its focus colour. The block is pieced on a newspaper foundation, and you can still see the newspaper's publication date – November 1938. It's amazing to me that, after all these years, this block is still inspiring quilters today.

In addition to the fabrics in the blocks, the fabrics in the border were stashbusters too. There was not enough of any one fabric that looked suitable, so I decided all of them would be used. The effect adds to the overall design, and keeps the viewer's eyes roving all over the quilt.

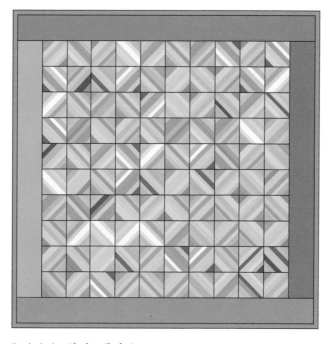

Basic String Block quilt design.

MEASUREMENTS

Quilt size:
72½ x 72½in (184.25 x 184.25cm)

Finished block size:
6in (15.25cm) square

REQUIREMENTS

Blocks:
Fabric strings, strips and scraps

Foundation:
130in (350cm) x WoF – I used a light-weight interfacing measuring 36in (91.5cm) wide

Focus colour (blue fabric):
I used shirts but you could use purchased fabric. If your fabric is purchased, based on 2in (5cm) wide strips as the widest cut, you'll need 56in (142.25cm) x WoF

Border:
45½in (115.75cm) x WoF of one fabric, or make this up from other fabrics. I used three in total. Look for fabrics that are similar in colour, scale of pattern and design

Wadding/batting:
82in (208.5cm) square

Backing:
162in (411.5cm) x WoF

Binding:
20in (51cm) x WoF

Notions:
6½in (16.5cm) square rotary-cutting ruler

FABRIC CUTTING

Blocks:
The total amount detailed under 'Requirements' is based on cutting twenty-eight 2in (5cm) wide strips x WoF.

My strips were cut at random widths that varied between 1¼in (3cm) and 2in (5cm). Remember that you can join odd strip lengths together to form new pieces, so you may not need all your total amount of fabric.

Foundation:
Cut twenty 6½in (16.5cm) strips x WoF, then sub-cut into one hundred 6½in (16.5cm) squares.

Remember that you can join the left-over foundation and you can use these too, to reduce the amount of foundation needed.

Focus colour (blue fabric):
Sub-cut the 2in (5cm) strips into one hundred 11in (28cm) pieces for each block, or keep the full length and chain piece.

Border:
Cut seven 6½in (16.5cm) strips x WoF. Remove the selvedge(s) and join the short ends to form a continuous length. Press the seams open.

Cut two 60½ x 6½in (153.75 x 16.5cm) strips.

Cut two 72½ x 6½in (184.25 x 16.5cm) strips.

Backing:
Cut into two equal lengths. Remove the selvedge(s), then join them RS together along one long edge. Press the seam open.

Binding:
Cut eight 2½in (6.5cm) x WoF strips. Join with bias joins to make a continuous length, then trim the SA to ¼in (5mm). Press the seams open. Press in half along the length, WS together.

METHOD

Step One Using the method detailed on pages 29–31, make one hundred string units. Start with your blue fabric strip in the middle of the diagonal on your foundation (see page 49).

Step Two I then stitched four units RS together to make a string block, with the blue strips forming a diamond-shaped design (**2a**). Stitch the units in pairs to start with, RS together, then sew two pairs RS together, pinning at the seam junction if needed. You can chain piece these blocks if you have lots of units ready to sew. Press the seams open. Make twenty-five blocks in total. Stitching them so the blue strips form a cross shape alters the emphasis of the overall pattern slightly (**2b**).

Step Three Lay out the blocks in five rows of five blocks, then stitch them RS together in rows. Press the seams open.

Step Four Stitch the rows RS together, pinning at the seam junctions if needed. Press the seams open.

Step Five Sew the short borders to the sides of the quilt. Press the seams towards the borders. Sew the remaining long borders to the top and bottom of the quilt. Again, press towards the borders.

Step Six Layer the quilt: place the backing RS down, centre the wadding/batting over the top, then centre the quilt top over these, RS up. Tack/baste the layers together, ready to quilt.

Step Seven To quilt, I big-stitch quilted in the ditch along both seams of the blue centre strips, and around the stripy wonky 'diamonds'. To make this process easy, quilt in one direction, right to left (left to right if you are left-handed), then skip to the next strip as needed. In addition, quilt ¼in (5mm) from the seam around the inner edge of the border. Then, in the border, mark a 45-degree cross-hatched grid, with the lines 1½in (3.75cm) apart. Quilt this with big-stitch quilting too.

Step Eight Once quilted, remove the tacking/basting stitches then trim the edges and square up. Bind the quilt with your chosen method (see pages 78–85), then finish with a label if you wish (see pages 86 and 87).

2a

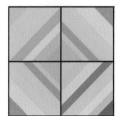

2b

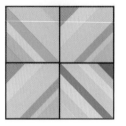

Half Log Cabin

Quilt size: 60½ x 60½in (153.75 x 153.75cm)

The block here puts paid to the idea that the pieces for Log Cabin blocks need to be cut and measured carefully. As long as you can trim and square up the finished blocks so they're all uniform in size, you can incorporate as many different widths of fabric strips and strings as you like.

This string quilt is a nod to the past, as I've used the traditional red square as the starting point for each block. Usually this would have been the centre of the block (supposedly representing the fire at the heart of the home), but here it is at the corner so that the red is more of a focal point. I've tried not to use red for the strings in the rest of the block, but I've used it in the binding to make the two coordinate.

I stitched one side of each block with the lighter fabrics first (see page 39); these first strips require less fabric, which I used to my advantage as I tend not to have many lighter-coloured fabrics in my stash. The darker, more colourful fabrics on the other side then become slightly more dominant as a result, making a stronger design. But, as with all string quilts, use what you have and make it work for you.

MEASUREMENTS

Quilt size:
60½ x 60½in (153.75 x 153.75cm)

Finished block size:
12in (30.5cm) square

REQUIREMENTS

Blocks:
Light and dark coloured scraps

Twenty-five 2½in (6.5cm) squares of red fabric –
I cut these from a 2½in (6.5cm) strip, by folding a
square and cutting by eye with scissors. You could
easily use up left-over squares cut for another quilt
or make the squares bigger

Wadding/batting:
70in (177.75cm) square

Backing:
142in (360.75cm) x WoF

Binding:
18in (45.75cm) x WoF

Notions:
12½in (31.75cm) square rotary-cutting ruler

FABRIC CUTTING

Backing:
Cut into two equal lengths, remove the selvedge(s)
and join along those edges. Press the seam open.

Binding:
Cut seven 2½in (6.5cm) x WoF strips. Join with bias
joins to make a continuous length, then trim the SA to
¼in (5mm). Press the seams open. Press in half along
the length, WS together.

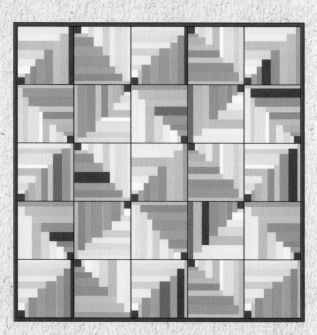

Half Log Cabin quilt design.

METHOD

Note: It's worth creating around sixteen blocks initially – before making up all twenty-five – so you can experiment with their arrangement: these blocks have a number of layout out options, and you may find you need more or fewer than I have used. So, have a play before deciding. The arrangement in **sample a** has a lovely, strong, diagonal design, and you could have a small sixteen-block quilt with large borders to extend the design. The layout for **sample b** is more unusual, and with more columns would make for an impressive repeat. Personally, for this layout I would have to stitch too many more blocks for my patience and scrap bag!

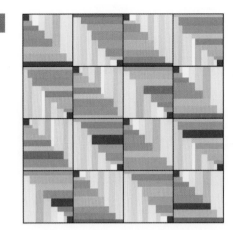

Step One Make up your Half Log Cabin blocks as described on page 39, starting with the red corner squares and stitching the light strings first. I made twenty-five in total for my quilt (see the note above if you'd like to make your quilt a little different to mine). They'll need to be approx. 13in (33in) square so they can be squared up to measure 12½in (31.75cm). Don't forget that you can chain piece on the machine for speedy progress, which will require less need to ponder fabric selection too. These blocks can be made up quickly by hand also, and are lovely projects to take with you when you're out and about.

Step Two Decide on your arrangement (see the note above). Once you decide on the layout, stitch the blocks RS together in rows. For my quilt, I had five rows of five blocks. Press the seams in each row in alternating directions.

Step Three Sew the rows RS together, knitting the seam junctions together. Press the long seams in one direction.

Step Four Layer the quilt: place the backing RS down, centre the wadding/batting over the top, then centre the quilt top over these, RS up. Tack/baste the layers together, ready to quilt.

Step Five This quilt was big-stitch quilted in a 45-degree diagonal grid (see the photograph on page 112). The lines were marked 2½in (6.5cm) apart, from the corner first. This utility-style quilting is in keeping with the ethos of the quilt, and does not take away from the patchwork design.

Step Six Once quilted, remove the tacking/basting stitches then trim the edges and square up. Bind the quilt with your chosen method (see pages 78–85), then finish with a label if you wish (see pages 86 and 87).

Wonky Squares

Quilt size: 76½ x 76½in (194.25 x 194.25cm)

This quilt was very much inspired by quilts in the collection of Roderick Kiracofe, shown in his book *Unconventional & Unexpected: American Quilts Below the Radar, 1950–2000* (Schiffer, 2022). Depending on where your eye focuses, you'll see bordered squares or mismatched crosses.

This quilt, as with lots of string quilts, is not about matching and accuracy. The strings are sewn onto a foundation then trimmed to shape and sewn into blocks. The mismatch and variation in the widths and angles of the fabric strips gives the quilt its quirky charm. Two triangles together will form the main block, and are part of the overall pattern, but it's not until four of these blocks are stitched together that you will see the wonky string squares appearing.

Using the same white fabric for the central strings of the triangles, with a navy string either side, not only unifies the quilt but ensures the wonky string squares are the focus. For your own quilt, you could also make sure the last strings you add at the corners of the triangles are the same colour or fabric (see 'Focus colours' on page 49). Both of these options add a different design element to the quilt, and help bring some of the randomness under a little more control.

The wide border helps frame the string design, the navy drawing your eye to the bordered squares. As the quilt is busy and I wanted the main design be the focal point, I've bound the quilt in the same fabric as the border, so there are no distractions.

If you love stitching these blocks, you can create a different design with the same triangles by stitching them together along the longest edges first. This creates smaller square units than the original design, and makes a quilt design with the grid on the diagonal.

Wonky Squares quilt design.

MEASUREMENTS

Quilt size:
76½ x 76½in (194.25 x 194.25cm)

Finished block size:
12in (30.5cm) square

REQUIREMENTS

Blocks:

Strings: full scrap bag of strings

OR you could use Jelly Roll pieces, cut as described in the instructions on page 25

Centre strip (white print): 40in (101.75cm) x WoF, based on cutting 2½in (6.5cm) wide strips

Framing strips (navy print): 36in (91.5cm) x WoF, based on strings measuring 7 x 1½in (17.75 x 3.75cm)

Foundation:
106in (270cm) x WoF – you might be able to get away with less, depending on how economically you cut. I used a light-weight, sew-in interfacing, which I always use as a foundation for my string quilts; however, feel free to use your own favourite interfacing or even newspaper, which can be torn away afterwards

Border:
68in (172.75cm) x WoF

Wadding/batting:
85in (216cm) square

Backing:
172in (437cm) x WoF

Binding:
20in (51cm) x WoF

Notions:
6 x 24in (15.25 x 61cm) rotary-cutting ruler

OR 6 x 12in (15.25 x 30.5cm) quilting ruler (like the one by Omnigrid®)

OR Quarter Square Triangle ruler

OR make your own template by cutting a 13¼in (33.5cm) square from piece of card or template plastic, sub-cut into four quarter square triangles then use one of these as your template

FABRIC CUTTING

Blocks:

Centre strip (white print): Cut sixteen strips that are a maximum of 2½in (6.5cm) wide x WoF, based on the yardage calculation left.

Framing strips (navy print): Cut twelve approx. 1½in (3.75cm) wide strips x WoF. You can vary the width of the strips, but if they are wider than 1½in (3.75cm) you may need more yardage. Sub-cut into one hundred and-twenty-eight 1½ x 7in (3.75 x 17.75cm) strips, or leave as is for chain piecing.

Foundation:
Cut eight 13¼in (33.75cm) wide strips x WoF. Sub-cut into sixteen 13¼in (33.5cm) squares. Sub-cut these each into four quarter square triangles.

Border:
Cut eight 8½in (21.75cm) strips x WoF. Remove the selvedge(s) and join the short ends to form a continuous length. Press the seams open.

Cut two 60½ x 8½in (153.75 x 21.75cm) strips.

Cut two 76½ x 8½in (194.25 x 21.75cm) strips.

Backing:
Cut into two equal lengths, remove selvedge(s) and join along those edges. Press the seam open.

Binding:
Cut eight 2½in (6.5cm) x WoF strips. Join with bias joins to make a continuous length, then trim the SA to ¼in (5mm). Press the seams open. Press in half along the length, WS together.

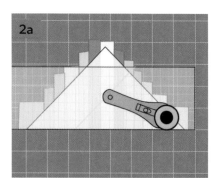

METHOD

Step One Piece the string triangles as on pages 29–31, using one white string for each centre, framing it with navy strips, then filling up the rest of the triangles with either your string scraps or sub-cut Jelly Rolls. Note that the strings need to stagger the edges of the foundation; these overlaps will be trimmed off later. Remember to press flat every two strings that are added; you will get a better finish. You could chain piece the strings for these triangles for speedier sewing.

Step Two Once all the triangles are stitched, trim the triangle back to size. Don't worry if the foundation has distorted; it is still doing its job, but you will need to trim the sewn piece to the correct size. I cut with the WS uppermost, so the foundation is visible. A turn-table cutting mat can be very useful too. Use either a template or triangle ruler the same size as your stitched triangles; alternatively, you can trim the shapes with a rectangular ruler. Here's how:

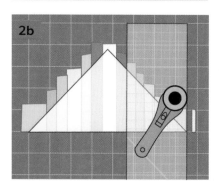

a) Place one stitched triangle on the cutting mat with the foundation side uppermost. Straighten the longest edge of the triangle with your ruler, using the foundation as a rough guide (as it's likely the foundation may have distorted a little after being stitched).

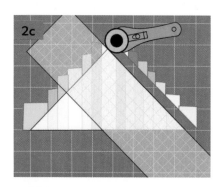

b) Align the trimmed edge with the straight horizontal line on the cutting mat, and one bottom 'corner' of the foundation with a vertical line. Measure from this end, to 13¼in (33.5cm). hen, trim off the excess fabric at the opposite bottom 'corner'.

c) At this cut corner, use the 45-degree angle on the ruler to position the ruler. Trim off the fabric at the angle.

d) Turn over the triangle and reposition it on a horizontal line. At the second corner, use the 45-degree angle on the ruler to trim this second side.

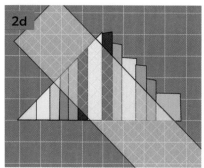

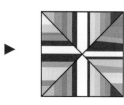

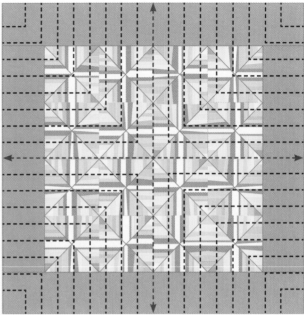

Step Three Now to 're-make' the square (also see the illustration opposite). When your triangles are trimmed, stitch them RS together in pairs to make a larger triangle, then press the seam open. Sew two pairs RS together to make a square/block. Press the seam open. Repeat to make sixteen blocks in total.

Step Four Arrange the squares in four rows of four. Stitch each row of blocks RS together then press the seams open.

Step Five Now join the rows RS together. Again, press the seams open.

Step Six Add the borders: stitch the short borders to the sides of the quilt then press the seams towards the borders. Stitch the long border to the remaining edges of the quilt. Again, press the seams towards the borders.

Step Seven Layer the quilt: place the backing RS down, centre the wadding/batting over the top, then centre the quilt top over these, RS up. Tack/baste the layers together, ready to quilt.

Step Eight This is very much a utility-style quilt, so the quilting design I've used is an expanded version of elbow quilting (see page 69). It goes from the quilt edge, over the border then into the main part of the quilt. I have quilted with big-stitch quilting; however, Mennonite tacks (see page 68) or machine stitching (see pages 74 and 75) would work equally well. Refer to the right-hand diagram above. Mark the quilt into four quarters (see the pink dashed arrows). Then, in each quarter, mark L-shape elbow quilting guide lines that are 2in (5cm) apart and 'radiate' from one corner – see the photograph and the black dashed marks in the diagram. Some of the lines will match up with the block seams; this will help guide you when you stitch.

Step Nine Once quilted, remove the tacking/basting stitches then trim the edges and square up. Bind the quilt with your chosen method (see pages 78–85), then finish with a label if you wish (see pages 86 and 87).

Stars + Spiders' Webs

Quilt size: 72½ x 72½in (184.25 x 184.25cm)

This design is a traditional one from the 1880s and uses up left-over scraps and strings from other quilts and garment making. Depending on how you place the colours and fabrics, you can change the design. Traditionally the 'stars' are in plain fabric, and then all of the 'webs' use scraps. However, by using a cream fabric for the outlines of the stars, it helps make them stand out in the quilt. It also means that you can use a print fabric for the stars, and it will not get lost in among the webs.

For my star fabric, I went for a print that has a lot of colours and a very large pattern. That way all of the stars look different, and the amount of colours helps balance out the variety of fabrics in the strings and scraps. The stars could be fussy cut, but you will need to calculate for more fabric if you do this. If you don't have enough of one particular fabric for the stars, it would be fun to make each one from a different fabric.

In the same way, using the same fabric for the star outline and border helps calm the quilt down. If you use the same fabric as I have here, then the stars and spiders' webs seem to float on the background. Another option is to use a print for the border, or a similar print to the star outline, but not the same. There are lots of ideas to play with and use up what you have. By making all of the outline strips varying widths, you'll give the spiders' webs a quirkiness if all of the sides do not line up.

For the binding, I used the same fabric for the stars as it gives the quilt a nice consistency.

Machine quilted by Chris Farrance.

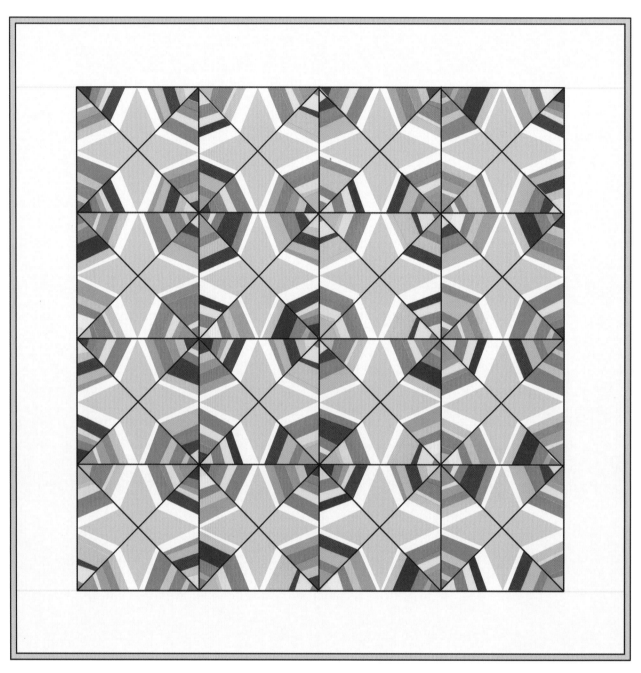

Stars + Spiders Webs quilt design.

MEASUREMENTS

Quilt size:
72½ x 72½in (184.25 x 184.25cm)

Finished block size:
15in (38.25cm) square

REQUIREMENTS

Spiders' webs (string octagons):
Use up all of your scraps and trimmings for this part. If you want to cut from yardage or Fat Quarters (22 x 18in/55 x 45cm), then remember to cut different widths, and that the strips do not need to be straight. If they are wider at one end than the other, this will add to the movement in the quilt

Stars (pink 'plain' pattern):
64in (162.5cm) x WoF

Outlines (cream):
52in (132cm) x WoF

Foundation:
132in (335.25cm) x WoF of sew-in light-weight interfacing – this will stay in the quilt and will not be removed

Border (cream):
45½in (115.75cm) x WoF

Wadding/batting:
82in (208.5cm) square

Backing:
164in (416.5cm) x WoF

Binding:
20in (51cm) x WoF

Notions:
Star template (see page 171)

Optional: fabric glue

FABRIC CUTTING

Stars:
Cut eight 8in (20.5cm) wide strips x WoF. Using the template, and ensuring the length of the stars fit across the width of the strips, cut sixty-four stars.

Outlines:
Cut 1–2in (2.5–5cm) wide strips x WoF, using the technique on page 25.

Foundation:
Cut sixteen 16¼in (41.25cm) squares, then sub-cut into sixty-four quarter square triangles.

Border:
Cut eight 6½in (16.5cm) strips x WoF. Remove the selvedge(s) and join the short ends to form a continuous length. Press the seams open.

Cut two 60½ x 6½in (153.75 x 16.5cm) strips.

Cut two 72½ x 6½in (184.25 x 16.5cm) strips.

Backing:
Cut into two equal lengths. Remove the selvedge(s), then join them RS together along one long edge. Press the seam open.

Binding:
Cut eight 2½in (6.5cm) x WoF strips. Join with bias joins to make a continuous length, then trim the SA to ¼in (5mm). Press the seams open. Press in half along the length, WS together.

METHOD

Step One Place a star piece on top of one triangle foundation, RS up; the raw edges will align at the top. You can pin this star piece or use a dab of fabric glue. I find that cotton fabric usually sticks to the interfacing by itself, so this is not always necessary.

Step Two Place an outline fabric strip along the raw edge of the star, RS together. Stitch along the right-hand edge, through both fabrics and the foundation, as shown. It is important that you start stitching before the foundation, and continue to stitch off the end of the strip, ¼in (5mm) away from the raw edge of the foundation. This will create a nice sharp point. Flip the strip to expose the RS and then press.

Step Three Now stitch another outline strip to the other side of the star, RS together. As before, start stitching before and after you touch the foundation. Flip and press.

Step Four Continue to fill in the rest of the foundation triangle in the same way, using the strings. Add a strip to each side before pressing; that way you can press the strips on both sides. When you get to the end 'corners', use larger scraps: if you use too small a piece, these will either get trimmed off or the SA will create too much bulk at the corners.

Step Five Repeat with the remaining star shapes, outline strips, strings and foundation triangles.

Step Six Now trim the triangles back to the right size, referring to step 2 of the Wonky Square quilt on page 120; the only difference is your long bottom edges should measure 16¼in (41.25cm) from one 'corner' to the other, rather than 13¼in (33.5cm). Remember to work from the WS to start with, so the foundation is visible. Sometimes the foundation will have shrunk up in the stitching process or have bowed. This will not matter.

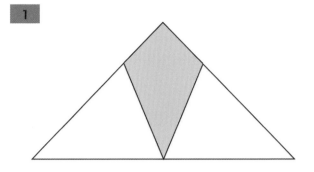
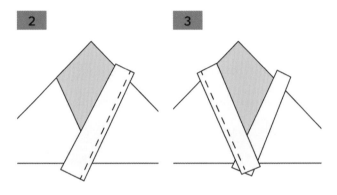
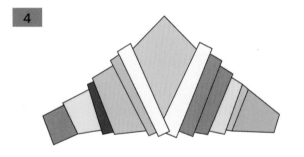
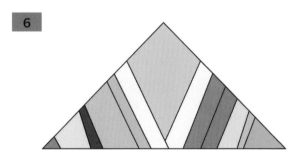

Step Seven Stitch the triangles RS together in pairs, along one of the shorter edges, to make a larger triangle. Press the seam open. Stitch two pairs RS together, along the longest edges. Press the seam open. Repeat to make sixteen blocks overall.

Step Eight Arrange the blocks in four rows of four blocks (see the diagram on page 124). Stitch the blocks in each row RS together. Press the seams open.

Step Nine Stitch the rows RS together. Press the seams open.

Step Ten Stitch the short borders to the sides of the quilt, RS together. Press the seams towards the borders. Stitch the long borders to the remaining top and bottom edges, again RS together. As before, press the seams towards the borders.

Step Eleven Layer the quilt: place the backing RS down, centre the wadding/batting over the top, then centre the quilt top over these, RS up. Tack/baste the layers together, ready to quilt.

Step Twelve This quilt was quilted all over on the machine with vermicelli stitching (see page 74). However, you could quilt by hand – outlining the stars with big-stitch quilting and tying the star centres. For big-stitch quilting, I recommend 12wt Coton Perle, as this fits nicely with the utilitarian nature of the quilt. Straight lines or cross-hatching would look good on the borders too.

Step Thirteen Once quilted, remove the tacking/basting stitches then trim the edges and square up. Bind the quilt with your chosen method (see pages 78–85), then finish off your quilt with a label if you wish (see pages 86 and 87).

7

Tulips + Picket Fences

Quilt size: 84½ x 84½in (215.5 x 215.5cm)

String-pieced tulips for piecing or appliqué are often seen in old string quilts and in blocks that never made it into quilts – see the examples on page 11. For this quilt, as a starting point I'd sewn a tulip block using a traditional pattern, but then didn't feel the urge to make yet more (perhaps that's how the makers of the vintage pieces felt too?). So, I decided to make my efforts the central feature in a framed/bordered quilt instead. String borders look great on the outside edge of a quilt, but when also repeated within the quilt they become a design feature in themselves. Borders made like this, in even-sized pieces, are often referred to as 'picket fence borders'. I think that is quite appropriate here – it's just a wonky fence around a patch of tulips!

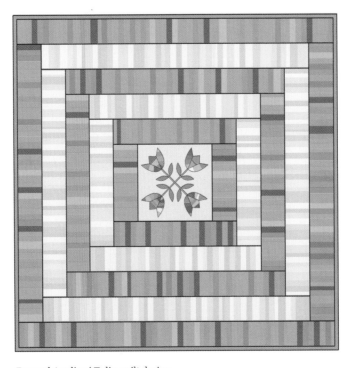

Framed Appliqué Tulip quilt design.

MEASUREMENTS

Quilt size:
84½ x 84½in (215.5 x 215.5cm)

Finished block size:
24½in (62.25cm) square

REQUIREMENTS

Tulip block:

Background: 25in (63.5cm) square

Stems: two 1¼ x 12½in (3¼ x 31.75cm) strips

Flowers and leaves:
one string-pieced fabric panel (see page 35) and
one Fat Eighth (9 x 22in/23 x 56cm)

Borders/frames:

Taupe: ten string-pieced fabric panels (see page 35),
each approx. 20 x 22in (50.75 x 56cm)

Cream: seven string-pieced fabric panels (see page 35),
each approx. 20 x 22in (50.75 x 56cm)

Wadding/batting:
94in (238.75cm) square

Backing:
168in (425.75cm) x WoF

Binding:
22½in (57.25cm) x WoF

Notions:

6½ x 24in (16.5 x 61cm) rotary-cutting ruler

Freezer paper, for appliqué

Templates A, B/BR and C (see page 169)

FABRIC CUTTING

Folding the stem piece.

Tulip block:

<u>Background:</u> press into quarters then into diagonals to crease, for placement of appliqué.

<u>Stems:</u> With the WS facing you, fold in the first long raw edge by a third, then fold the remaining long raw edge over to meet the first fold (so you have three layers of fabric). Turn the piece so the raw edge is 'hidden' at the back. Make two. (See the two diagrams above.)

<u>Flowers and leaves:</u> using the templates, cut the following pieces from freezer paper: four A, four B, four BR, eight C.

Iron the shiny sides of the shapes onto the WS of the string-pieced panel, allowing at least ½in (1.25cm) of space between each shape. Cut out the shapes, adding a ¼in (5mm) SA all round. Tack/baste the SAs to the WS (see page 41).

Borders/frames:
<u>Taupe:</u>

Cut thirty 6½ x 22in (16.5 x 56cm) strips from the panels. Join to make a continuous length and cut:

Taupe 1: two 6½ x 24½in (16.5 x 62.25cm) strips and two 6½ x 36½in (16.5 x 92.75cm) strips

Taupe 2: two 6½ x 48½in (16.5 x 123.25cm) strips and two 6½ x 60½in (16.5 x 153.75cm) strips

Taupe 3: two 6½ x 72½in (16.5 x 184.25cm) strips and two 6½ x 84½in (16.5 x 214.75cm) strips

<u>Cream:</u>

Cut twenty 6½ x 22in (16.5 x 56cm) from the panels. Join to make a continuous length and cut:

Cream 1: two 6½ x 36½in (16.5 x 92.75cm) strips and two 6½ x 48½in (16.5 x 123.25cm) strips

Cream 2: two 6½ x 60½in (16.5 x 153.75cm) strips and two 6½ x 72½in (16.5 x 184.25cm) strips

Backing:
Cut into two equal lengths. Remove the selvedge(s), then join them RS together along one long edge. Press the seam open.

Binding:
Cut nine 2½in (6.5cm) x WoF strips. Join with bias joins to make a continuous length, then trim the SA to ¼in (5mm). Press the seams open. Press in half along the length, WS together.

METHOD

Step One For the central appliqué block, fold each stem piece in half, to crease the centre, then unfold and position the two stems along each diagonal, the creases of their halfway points overlapping and crossing each other. Make sure the side with the long raw edge faces the quilt. Pin then sew them in place with appliqué stitch/slip stitch.

Step Two Stitch a B and a BR piece to either side of an A piece, RS together and using whip/over-edge stitch (as you would for English Paper Piecing). Repeat to make four tulip flowers in total.

Step Three Position a tulip flower at the end of each stem, overlapping the raw edge by about ½in (1.25cm). Pin and sew in place with appliqué stitch (see pages 44 and 45). With each flower, start from one long edge then, when you are close to your starting point, leave a 1in (2.5cm) gap. Remove any tacking/basting stitches and freezer papers, then complete the appliqué.

Step Four Position two leaves halfway up each stem, on either side. Pin and sew with appliqué stitch as before, starting and stopping on a curved edge and making sure to finish just shy of your starting point so you can remove the freezer papers.

Step Five Trim and square up the background panel to measure 24½in (62.25cm) square.

Step Six Add the first border pieces, starting with the Taupe 1 border strips. Stitch the two shortest Taupe 1 strips to the sides of the central block, RS together. Press the SAs towards the block. Sew the longer Taupe 1 border strips to the top and bottom edges, RS together. Press as before.

Step Seven Repeat to add the second border pieces to the framed central block, using the shorter Cream 1 strips for the sides and the longer Cream 1 strips for the top and bottom edges. Press as before.

Step Eight Always starting with the shorter strips for the sides and finishing with the longer strips for the top and bottom edges, use the same method to add the remaining borders: Taupe 2, Cream 2, Taupe 3.

Step Nine Layer the quilt: place the backing RS down, centre the wadding/batting over the top, then centre the quilt top over these, RS up. Tack/baste the layers together, ready to quilt.

Step Ten Mark the quilting for the centre panel: measure 2in (5cm) in from the seams on all four sides. Repeat, working from the marked line towards the centre of the quilt, the marked squares getting smaller and smaller in size. Continue until you've made five circuits in the total, and have a small 'square' at the centre of the quilt. Note the markings will go over the appliqué too. Mark the borders in 2in (5cm) increments also.

Step Eleven Quilt Mennonite tacks along the marked lines (see page 68), and in the ditches of the border seams.

Step Twelve Once quilted, remove the tacking/basting stitches trim the edges and square up. Bind the quilt with your chosen method (see pages 78–85), then finish with a label if you wish (see pages 86 and 87).

Vintage Embroidered Tablecloths

Quilt size: 64½ x 64½in (163.75 x 163.75cm)

This quilt makes the most of old embroidered linens that might have fallen out of favour or fashion as everyday household linens.

Many vintage tablecloths and linens are consigned to the backs of cupboards because they have become stained or damaged, yet haven't been discarded as they still have sentimental value. I collect a lot of mine from charity/thrift/op shops where they can often be purchased for very little money.

The fabric that I chose from my stash for the cornerstones/posts was not quite enough, so some of the cornerstones/posts are pieced together from off-cuts of that fabric to make a piece big enough. If I'd run out of that fabric completely, substituting from my stash would have been my next step.

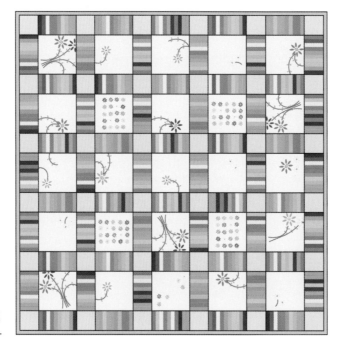

Vintage Embroidered Tablecloths quilt design.

MEASUREMENTS

Quilt size:
64½ x 64½in (163.75 x 163.75cm)

Finished block size:
8in (20.25cm) square

REQUIREMENTS

Blocks:
Two to three coordinating embroidered table linens or tray cloths – the number will depend on their condition, as if there are stains or holes then these might need to be cut around. It will also depend on how much of the cloth is actually embroidered. Often there are large pieces that are blank, and you can decide whether you want to incorporate these into the quilt too

Sashing:
This is made from string fabric (see page 35). I usually make my new fabric in pieces about 20 x 22in (51 x 56cm). Based on this, about eight panels of string fabric would do

Cornerstones/posts:
22½in (57.25cm) x WoF

Wadding/batting:
74in (188cm) square

Backing:
148in (376cm) x WoF

Binding:
17½in (44.5cm) x WoF

Notions:
8½in (21.5cm) square rotary-cutting ruler, or a larger one if a substitute is needed

FABRIC CUTTING

Blocks:
Cut twenty-five 8½in (21.75cm) squares from your various linens.

Depending on the linen selected, you may have lots of embroidery motifs you want to fussy cut, or you may decide to cut the cloth into strips then sub-cut these into squares, which will result in a more random selection of motifs. Some of my panels ended up being pieced together to make them big enough to use, in true patchwork fashion.

Sashing:
Cut sixty 4½ x 8½in (11.5 x 21.75cm) rectangles.

I cut 4½in (11.5cm) wide strips from my strip fabric, then sub-cut these into 8½in (21.75cm) rectangles. Any left-over pieces can be joined together and then re-cut.

Cornerstones/posts:
Cut five 4½in (11.5cm) x WoF strips, then sub-cut into thirty-six 4½in (11.5cm) squares.

Backing:
Cut into two equal lengths. Remove the selvedge(s), then join them RS together along one long edge. Press the seam open.

Binding:
Cut seven 2½in (6.5cm) x WoF strips. Join with bias joins to make a continuous length, then trim the SA to ¼in (5mm). Press the seams open. Press in half along the length, WS together.

'Grid' quilting.

METHOD

Note: The quilt is constructed by piecing two types of rows – one made up of sashing and cornerstones/posts (Row A), the other squares of embroidered linen and sashing (Row B). You might want to arrange the embroidery into a pleasing layout before sewing it into the quilt. For my quilt, I cut up a tablecloth that had a circular motif and tried to re-create the circular design when I put it into the quilt top.

Step One Start with a row made of only sashing and cornerstones/posts (Row A). Stitch six cornerstones/posts and five string rectangles RS together, along the short edges of the rectangles. Make sure to start and end with a cornerstone/post, and to sew the cornerstones/posts and rectangles alternately. Press the seams towards the posts. Repeat to make six Row A rows in total.

Step Two Sew a row made of only blocks (linen squares) and sashing (Row B). Stitch six string rectangles and five squares of embroidered linen RS together, along the longer edges of the string rectangles. Make sure to start and end with a string rectangle, and to sew the rectangles and squares of embroidered linen alternately. Press the seams towards the linen squares. Repeat to make five Row B rows in total.

Step Three Arrange the Row A and Row B rows together, starting and finishing with a Row A. Pin the rows RS together, especially pinning at the post and block junctions where the seams knit together. Sew, then press seams towards the linen blocks (Row B).

Step Four Layer the quilt: place the backing RS down, centre the wadding/batting over the top, then centre the quilt top over these, RS up. Tack/baste the layers together, ready to quilt.

Step Five This quilt is easily quilted by hand or machine with simple straight lines. Quilt ¼in (5mm) from either side of the sashing and block seams. These extend across the length and width of the quilt, which means you can quilt in a continuous line from one side to the other. Three-by-three grids are then marked inside each block (linen square); as with the block and sashing seams, these can be quilted in continuous lines across the length and width of the quilt (see the bottom-right photograph opposite).

Step Six Once quilted, remove the tacking/basting stitches then trim the edges and square up. Bind the quilt with your chosen method (see pages 78–85), then finish with a label if you wish (see pages 86 and 87).

1   Row A:

2   Row B:

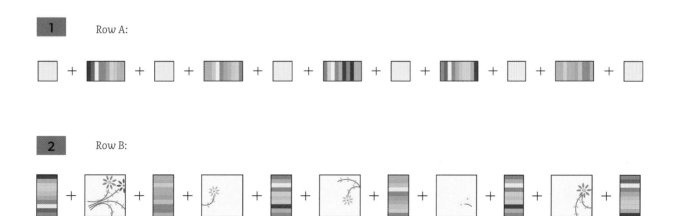

Housetop Sawtooth Star

Quilt size: 82 x 82in (208.25 x 208.25cm)

This is a true scrap quilt and, in fact, its instructions are more of a recipe for you to adapt and adjust, depending on what your fabric allows: because it is built up by adding strips of whatever width you like around a central panel, it is easy to make it any size you like.

The inspiration behind this quilt comes from African American quiltmakers. It's a design that begins with a central motif, to 'anchor' the quilt, that is then surrounded by borders and frames that radiate from it. It is a style of quilt also often named 'Pig Pen' as well as 'Housetop'. It is not always clear why these names came to be. Perhaps the centre represents the home and the frames the surrounding fences? Other quiltmakers would see this quilt as a variation on the Log Cabin and Courthouse Steps blocks. The differing interpretations go to show that it is the continuing evolvement of these designs in a quiltmaker's hands that keeps things new and fresh. Furthermore, it is your fabrics and fabric choices that make classic quilts exciting, individual and personal.

I had started with a single Sawtooth Star block, made out of one of my favourite fabric combinations, with the intention of making a quilt wholly with these stars. However, I then felt I didn't want to lose these much-loved fabrics in a quilt of stars. So, I decided to make the single star a focal point and frame it in the centre of its own quilt. The fabrics that surround the star are from a stash with a similar colour palette, and so include lots of different shades as well as scales of prints. This variation of fabrics, I think, is what makes the quilt so fun to look at.

As I was framing the star, I found I was running out of fabrics. However, I just added another pattern to the mix, which goes to show it really will not matter if you run out of something.

MEASUREMENTS

Quilt size:
82 x 82in (208.25 x 208.25cm)

Finished block size:
12in (30.5cm) square

REQUIREMENTS

Star block:
Centre: 6½ x 6½in (16.5 x 16.5cm)

Points: 4 x 18in (10 x 45.75cm)

Background: 8 x 18in (20.25 x 45.75cm)

Strips:
Yardage totalling 98½–140in (250–350cm) x WoF

Use as many fabrics as you can – twenty or more is ideal to avoid repeats

Wadding/batting:
92in (233.75cm) square

Backing:
184in (467.5cm) x WoF

Binding:
22½in (57.25cm) x WoF

Notions:
Optional: Amish Wave template (see page 175)

FABRIC CUTTING

Star block:
Centre: one 6½in (16.5cm) square

Points: four 3⅞in (9.75cm) squares. Sub-cut each square across one diagonal to make eight Half Square Triangles (HST) in total.

Background: four 3½in (9cm) squares, one 7¼in (18.5cm) square. Sub-cut the 7¼in (18.5cm) square across both diagonals to make four Quarter Square Triangles (QST) in total.

Strips:
Cut the fabrics into 1½– 2½in (3.75– 6.5cm) wide x WoF strips. You can trim off the selvedge as you sew.

Backing:
Cut into two equal lengths. Remove the selvedge(s), then join them RS together along one long edge. Press the seam open.

Binding:
Cut nine 2½in (6.5cm) x WoF strips. Join with bias joins to make a continuous length, then trim the SA to ¼in (5mm). Press the seams open. Press in half along the length, WS together.

Housetop Sawtooth Star quilt design.

METHOD

Step One Start with the centre star. Place a point piece (HST) over one side of a QST background fabric, RS together and matching up the similar angles – there will be an overhang at the bottom. Sew along the shorter edge, as shown, then press the seam away from the background fabric.

Step Two Now add a second point to the other short edge of the same QST background piece as in step 1. Again, press the seam away from the background fabric as before. One flying-geese unit made. Make four of these units in total.

Step Three On either side of one of the flying-geese units, sew a background square RS together. Press the seams towards the squares. Repeat to make two of these units in total.

Step Four Stitch the remaining flying-geese units to either side of the centre square, RS together. Press the seams towards the centre square.

Step Five Stitch the two units made in step 3 to the top and bottom of the centre square unit, RS together. Press the seams towards the centre square unit. This is the central design of star the quilt.

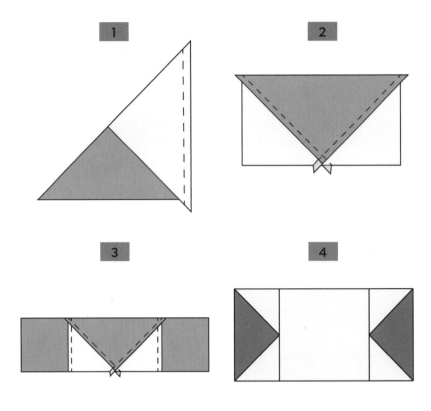

Step Six Starting on any side of the central square, sew any of the strips RS together along one side. Trim the strip at the end of the block. Finger-press the end of the seam towards the strip.

Step Seven Now add a second strip, starting at the end of the first strip, as you would when making a Log Cabin block (see page 37). Trim and finger-press as before. Add a third strip to the third side in the same way; trim and finger press. On the fourth side do the same. Once four strips are sewn, press the whole bordered square with an iron. All of the seams are pressed away from the centre of the quilt.

Step Eight Continue adding 'rounds' in this way, Log-Cabin style, until the quilt is the desired size. For best results, finger-press after adding each strip then press with an iron when the round is complete, as above. This is a very scrappy quilt, so the strip width I chose for each round were selected based on what 'felt right'. Try to stitch each round with strips of the same width to keep it square. If you find your strips aren't quite long enough as the quilt gets larger, just stitch two strips together and press the seams open. Don't worry about joining different fabrics together if you do this; I think it makes the quilt more interesting if there are different fabrics in a similar tone, and you will not have to worry about running out of a particular fabric.

Step Nine When the desired size is obtained, layer the quilt: place the backing RS down, centre the wadding/batting over the top, then centre the quilt top over these, RS up. Tack/baste the layers together, ready to quilt.

Step Ten For this quilt, I big-stitched Amish Waves freehand (see pages 70 and 71); you could use a template for this, which will make a smaller quilting pattern – see the one on page 175.

Step Eleven Once quilted, remove the tacking/basting stitches then trim the edges and square up. Bind the quilt with your chosen method (see pages 78–85), then finish with a label if you wish (see pages 86 and 87).

THE PROJECTS

Gifts + accessories

Selvedge-edge Scrap Basket

Finished size: 12 x 12 x 10in (30.5 x 30.5 x 25.5cm)

I love the idea that this basket holds scraps and is stitched from scraps – everything coming full circle. The 'stitch-and-flip' method (see page 29) makes this a sturdy basket with very little sewing involved. You can adapt the design to make the basket bigger or smaller by using different-sized squares for the sides and base.

REQUIREMENTS

Outer:
Selvedges from fabrics and a small selection of strings

As I had only enough selvedge pieces for the sides, I used a single coordinating fabric for the outer base since this would be hidden from view. If, like me, you have only a small collection of selvedge pieces, you will need a 13in (33cm) square of regular fabric for the outer base panel

Lining:
The lining can be all one fabric or made up of oddments. If you choose one fabric, you will need 26in (66cm) x WoF

Wadding/batting:
For the base, one 13in (33cm) square of sew-in foam interfacing for structure and stability

For the sides, four 13in (33cm) squares of regular wadding/batting

Lining seam bindings:
The binding can be all one fabric or made up of oddments. If you choose one fabric, you will need 4½in (11.5cm) x WoF

Top-edge binding:
As above, if you choose one fabric you will need 5in (12.75cm) x WoF

Notions:
Fabric clips

Hera marker

FABRIC CUTTING

Lining:
If you are using one fabric, cut two 13in (33cm) strips x WoF then sub-cut into five 13in (33cm) squares

Lining seam bindings:
Cut three 1½in (3.75cm) x WoF strips. Join to make a continuous length with bias joins. Trim the SAs to ¼in (5mm) then press open. Score a crease ¼in (5mm) from one long edge, all along the length, on the WS.

Top-edge binding:
Cut two 2½in (6.5cm) wide x WoF strips. Join to make a continuous length with bias joins. Trim the SAs to ¼in (5mm) then press open. Press the long edges WS together.

METHOD

Step One Place a lining square WS up in front of you then centre a wadding/batting square on top. Use this as your foundation. Make up a selvedge-pieced square (see page 33). Repeat three more times to create four side panels in total. Trim each to measure 12½in (31.75cm).

Step Two Make up the layers for the base of the basket: sandwich the foam between the WS of the remaining lining square and the base piece. As noted, I used one plain 13in (33cm) square for my base piece; however, you could piece the base with selvedge strips if you wish. If you'd prefer a selvedge-pieced base, make it at this stage. Otherwise, machine stitch two diagonal lines on your fabric square, working from the RS of the lining fabric and stitching corner to corner, to hold the three layers together. Trim to measure 12½in (31.75cm). To keep the edges in place for the next step, sew zigzag stitch around the outside edge.

Step Three To construct the basket, lay one side panel over the basket base, RS together. Lay the lining seam binding strip on top, RS together and raw edges aligned, and with the creased edge furthest from the seam. Stitch with a ¼in (5mm) SA, holding the three layers together with fabric clips. Trim off the excess binding tape at the ends of the seam.

Step Four Turn under the creased edge, then fold the binding over the raw edge. This should overlap the machine stitching of the seam. Using fabric clips to hold the strip in place, machine sew the binding in place, close to the folded edge and in the ditch of the original seam.

Step Five Repeat with a second panel and a lining seam binding strip on the opposite side of the basket.

2

3

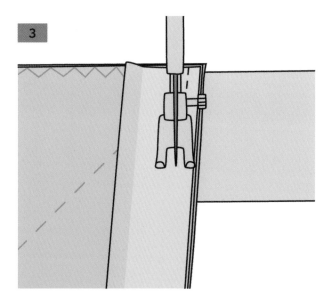

4

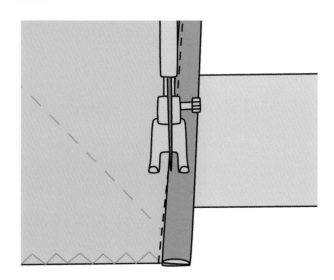

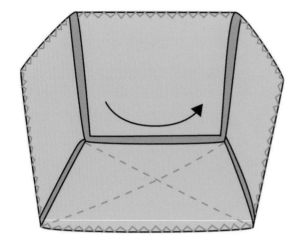

6

Step Six To attach the third panel, follow a similar procedure but sew the binding along the sides and base as one continuous seam, starting from one top edge of the side panel, sewing across the base then up the other side (see the direction of the arrow in the illustration). Snip into the lining seam binding at the corners when you turn.

Step Seven Repeat on the remaining side with the fourth panel and remaining binding strip.

Step Eight To finish, bind the top raw edge as you would a quilt. I used the mock bias finish to conceal the ends (see page 80), bound the basket from the lining side then slip-stitched the folded edge on the front/selvedge side of the basket. This way, when the top edge of the basket is turned over to make a cuff, it is the cleaner machined edge you see. As you work, fold the bound seams in one direction to help them lie flat.

Tiled + Quilted Shirt-backed Pillow

Finished size: 16in (40.5cm) square

The size of this pillow or cushion is very much decided by the square that you can cut from a shirt front, so yours may be bigger or smaller. I had a pocket on the shirt and this is a fun addition for children to pop in a favourite toy or for adults to keep the TV control in!

For the front I used a variation on the 'Tile block' crumb technique on page 78. However, you can choose one of any of the crumb designs for your own for your pillow front, or have a selection.

Keep to a colour theme to help your pillow have cohesive look, and use one fabric's colour as a starting point for the selection of others. If you have a few pieces of that fabric to repeat here and there in the pillow front, that will help too.

REQUIREMENTS

Pillow back:
One shirt – note its size will dictate the sizes for the rest of the pillow

Pillow front background:
17in (43.25cm) square of linen/cotton mix fabric – the size may vary, depending on the shirt

Pillow front 'tiles':
Fabric scraps

Wadding/batting:
18in (45.75cm) square of wadding/batting

OR 18in (45.75cm) square of cotton flannel

Lining:
18in (45.75cm) square of your chosen fabric – mine was the same as the pillow-front background

Notions:
17in (43.25cm) square pillow insert – this may vary, depending on the size of the shirt

Hera marker or chalk and quilt ruler, for marking

Optional: fabric glue

METHOD

Step One To determine the size of the pillow, cut your shirt front into a square while it's buttoned up – the narrowest measurement across the chest will dictate this. Press and set aside. Hold on to the other parts of the shirt for use in future projects.

Step Two For the pillow front, lay out the lining WS up, centre the wadding/ batting or cotton flannel over this, then centre the pillow front background on top, RS up. Tack/baste the layers together.

Step Three On the pillow-front background, mark a square that's 1in (2.5cm) smaller all around – I used a Hera marker. This will keep the tile scraps out of the side seams, and help with squaring up afterwards. With the RS facing up, arrange the fabric crumbs/tile scraps within the outline. Leave spaces between the scraps, to act as 'grouting'. When you are happy with the layout either pin or use fabric glue to keep the pieces in place before you start to sew.

Step Four The tile scraps are secured with matchstick quilting (see page 74). I marked my first stitch line through the middle of the pillow front. Machine quilt through all the layers. You may like to use a longer stitch than your usual stitch length; experiment to see what you like. Proceed to quilt parallel lines that are in ⅛–¼in (3–5mm) apart. Matchstick quilting will not only hold the pieces in place, and secure the layers below too, but also add texture. If you've used pins to temporarily secure the scraps, remove them as you approach them.

Step Five Once all the scraps are secure and the whole pillow front is quilted, square up and trim the panel square to measure the same size as your pillow insert – mine is 17in (43.25cm) square.

Step Six Place the pillow back (the shirt front cut in Step One) and quilted front RS together and pin around the outside edge. Sew around the edges with a ½in (1.25cm) SA. Notice in the diagram below that I worked a couple of stitches diagonally across the corners, which makes the corners look neater when turned through.

Step Seven Trim across the corners at a diagonal angle to remove bulk (see the illustration below left) then stitch zigzag or overcast stitch on your sewing machine around the raw edges to neaten.

Step Eight Undo the shirt front and turn the pillow cover RS out. Poke out the corners so they're nice and sharp. Push the pillow insert inside the cover then do up the buttons to finish.

7

Tulip Table Runner

Finished size: 12½ x 48½in (31.75 x 123.25cm)

Sometimes what you have dictates what you make. The tea towels used for the block background were originally bought for the kitchen, and I loved the graphic black-and-white pattern. It seemed a fun idea to use some colourful scraps and make a coordinating runner for the table.

The size of the block was determined by the size of the tea towels: I wanted to use as much of the towel in the block as possible. The strip that was cut off from the two tea towels would be great for coaster backings, or you could join off-cuts together to make more blocks.

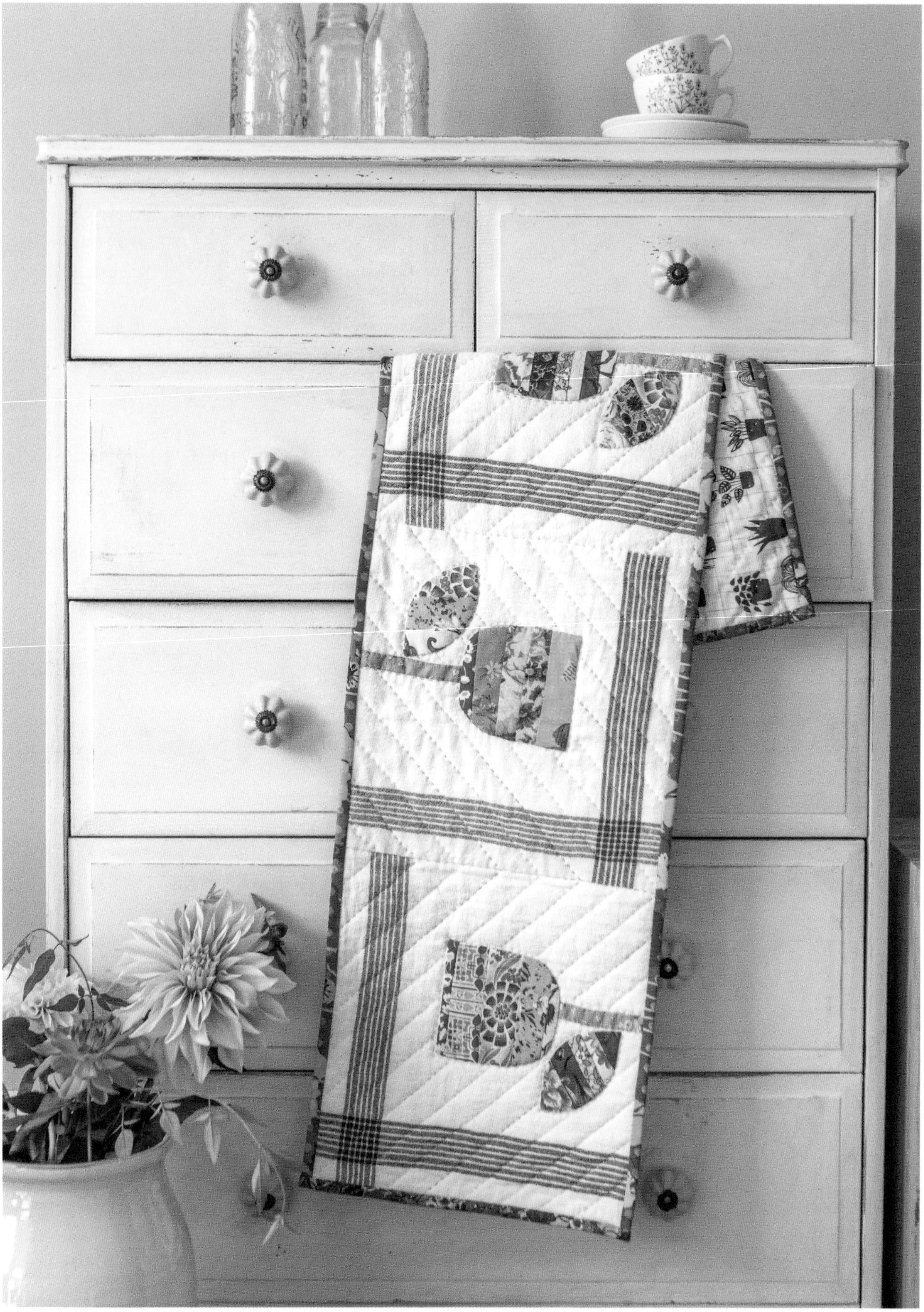

MEASUREMENTS

Finished block size:
12in (30.5cm) square

REQUIREMENTS

Background:
Two tea towels – mine were 26 x 19in
(66 x 48.25cm)

OR 25in (63.5cm) x WoF

Tulip and leaves:
Approx. 20 x 22in (50.75 x 56cm) of string fabric
(see page 35)

Stem:
Four 1½ x 5in (3.75 x 12.75cm) strips

Backing:
32in (81.25cm) x WoF

Wadding/batting:
52 x 16in (132 x 40.75cm)

Binding:
10in (26cm) x WoF

OR Four 2½in (6.5cm) x WoF

Interfacing:
5in (12.75cm) x WoF of sew-in or iron-on
light-weight interfacing

Notions:
Tulip and Leaf templates (see page 168)

Pencil, for drawing on interfacing

FABRIC CUTTING

Background:
Cut four 12½in (31.75cm) squares.

Backing:
Cut two 16in (40.5cm) x WoF strips.

Binding:
Cut four 2½in (6.5cm) wide x WoF strips. Join to
make a continuous length with bias joins. Trim the
SAs to ¼in (5mm) then press open. Press the long
edges WS together.

Interfacing:
Cut four 5in (12.75cm) squares and four 5 x 2¾in
(12.75 x 7cm) rectangles.

METHOD

Step One On each 5in (12.75cm) interfacing square, draw around the tulip template; repeat with the leaf template on the interfacing rectangles. Follow the 'Interfaced appliqué method on pages 42 and 43 to create four tulips and four leaves with neat edges.

Step Two Make the stems by folding the strip into thirds along the length and pressing flat (see the diagrams on page 131). Make sure the raw edge is hidden at the back.

Step Three Position the flower, leaf and stem on each background square. Note the leaf position in the photograph on page 155, or play around with a balance that you like. You can see how I placed mine so the base of the stem is flush with one edge of the background square, and so the whole flower is within the frame of the woven plaid. If you have a more evenly balanced fabric, arrange each flower in the centre of one side. Pin in place and appliqué down by hand, as described on pages 44 and 45. If you have iron-on interfacing, you can iron them into position so that there is no need to pin.

Step Four Stitch the appliquéd squares RS together in a row of four. Choose a layout that you like or follow mine (where every second flower square is facing in the opposite direction). Press the seams in alternate directions. Trim off any overhanging stems so they are neatly in line with the square edge.

Step Five Layer the quilt: place the backing RS down, centre the wadding/batting over the top, then centre the quilt top over these, RS up. Tack/baste the layers together, ready to quilt.

Step Six To quilt, I hand stitched in the ditch between each block with big-stitch quilting. I then quilted around each flower, stem and leaf, ⅛in (3mm) from the shapes. Next I marked diagonal lines across each block, the lines 1in (2.5cm) apart and starting from the centre of the block. I made sure to alternate the direction of the diagonal lines in each block, to create a zigzag pattern along the runner. Note, I didn't stitch over the appliqué.

Step Seven Once quilted, remove the tacking/basting stitches then trim the backing and wadding/batting in line with the patchwork top. Bind with square-cornered binding (see page 84).

Snowball Pincushion

Finished size: 8in (20.25cm) square

The left-over quarter circles from Snowball blocks (see the quilt on pages 96–101) always offer lots of ideas for stitching creativity.

Here, I've showcased the fabrics in the centre of this useful pincushion. If you wanted to use more of them together, sew nine of these blocks into a fun cushion.

This is much larger than the standard pincushion, which is handy when you are sewing large projects like quilts, and need somewhere to place your pins when chain-piecing.

REQUIREMENTS

Pincushion front:
Four quarter circles left-over from Snowball blocks (see page 99), for the circular motif

8½in (21.5cm) square of linen, for the background

Wadding/batting:
10in (25.5cm) square

Backing fabric:
Two 8½ x 4¾in (21.5 x 12cm) rectangles of fabric

Notions:
Stuffing, for filling

Optional: Hera marker and quilt ruler, for marking

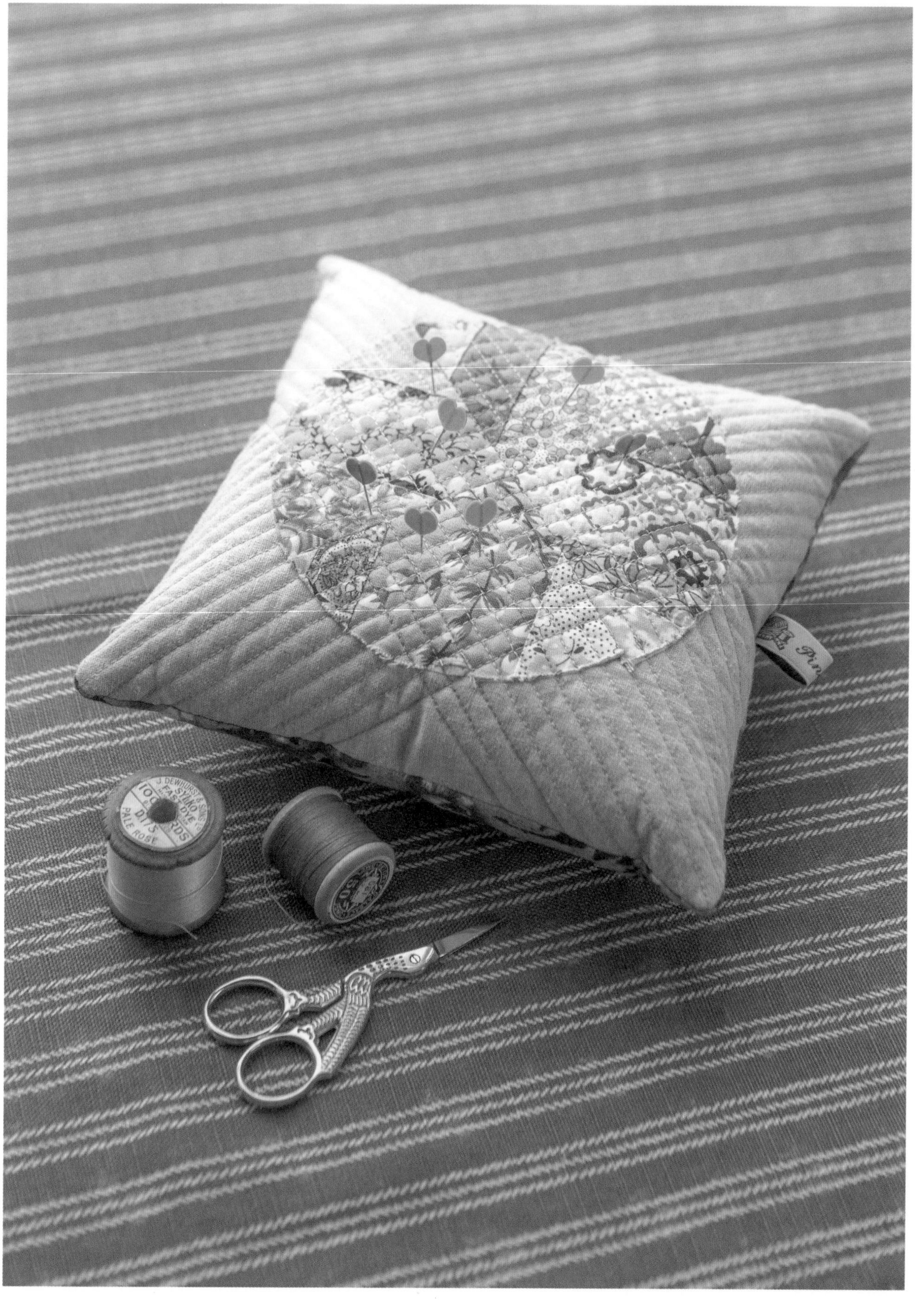

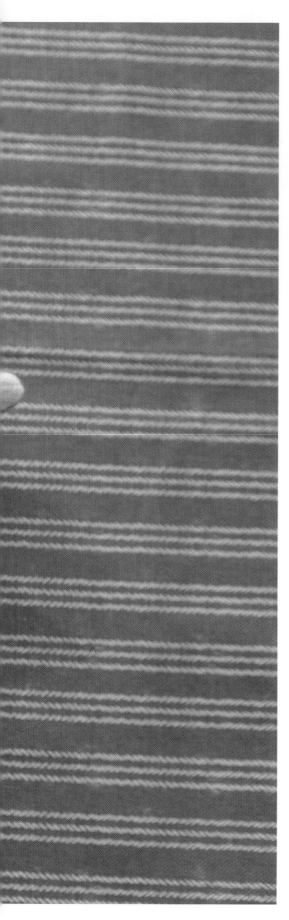

METHOD

Step One Stitch the quarter circles RS together in pairs to make two half circles. Press the seams open. Stitch the two halves RS together to make a circle. Press the seam open.

Step Two Place the circle centrally over the RS of the linen square, then place both centrally over the wadding/batting. Pin or tack/baste the layers together.

Step Three Quilt the layers together – I've used matchstick quilting (see page 74), which creates straight lines for the linen and cross-hatched lines for the circle. Start with the diagonal in each direction, working from one corner to the opposite corner. Stitch lines ¼in (5mm) apart. I stitch and turn the work after each line, so I'm systematically quilting on each side and direction as I work. I stopped when I was happy that all the circle was securely quilted in place.

Step Four Square up and trim the pincushion front to measure 8½in (21.5cm) square.

Step Five Stitch the two pieces of backing fabric RS together along the 8½in (21.5cm) side with a ½in (1.25cm) SA, leaving a 1½in (3.75cm) gap in the centre of the seam. Press the seam open.

Step Six Place the backing panel and quilted pincushion front RS together and pin. At this point, you may wish to tuck a label into the seam if you wish, as I did. If you do this, make sure the ends of the label match the raw edge of the pincushion back or front, and that it faces inwards. Stitch all around the outside edge. Cut across the corners (taking care not to snip into the stitching) to remove bulk (see the illustration on page 153), then turn RS out through the gap in the seam.

Step Seven Poke out the corners to make them sharp. Stuff the pincushion and stitch the gap closed.

Thread-saver Gift Tags + Notecards

Finished sizes: as desired – I use 2 x 3in (5 x 7.5cm) pieces of paper or card for the gift tags and A6 (4¼ x 5¾in/ 105 x 148mm) cards for the notecards

I'd always been happy to use my thread savers until they were full, and then bin them, until someone mentioned that they would be a great foundation for an embroidery and textile collage.

So, now there is another tin by my sewing machine to house thread savers. When the time is right, and my thread savers are covered in thread, gift tags or notecards can be conjured very quickly.

Thread savers combine really well with odd bits of vintage embroidered fabric that are too small for sewing with, but too precious to discard; similarly, they're ideal for using up buttons and beads when there aren't enough to use in a project.

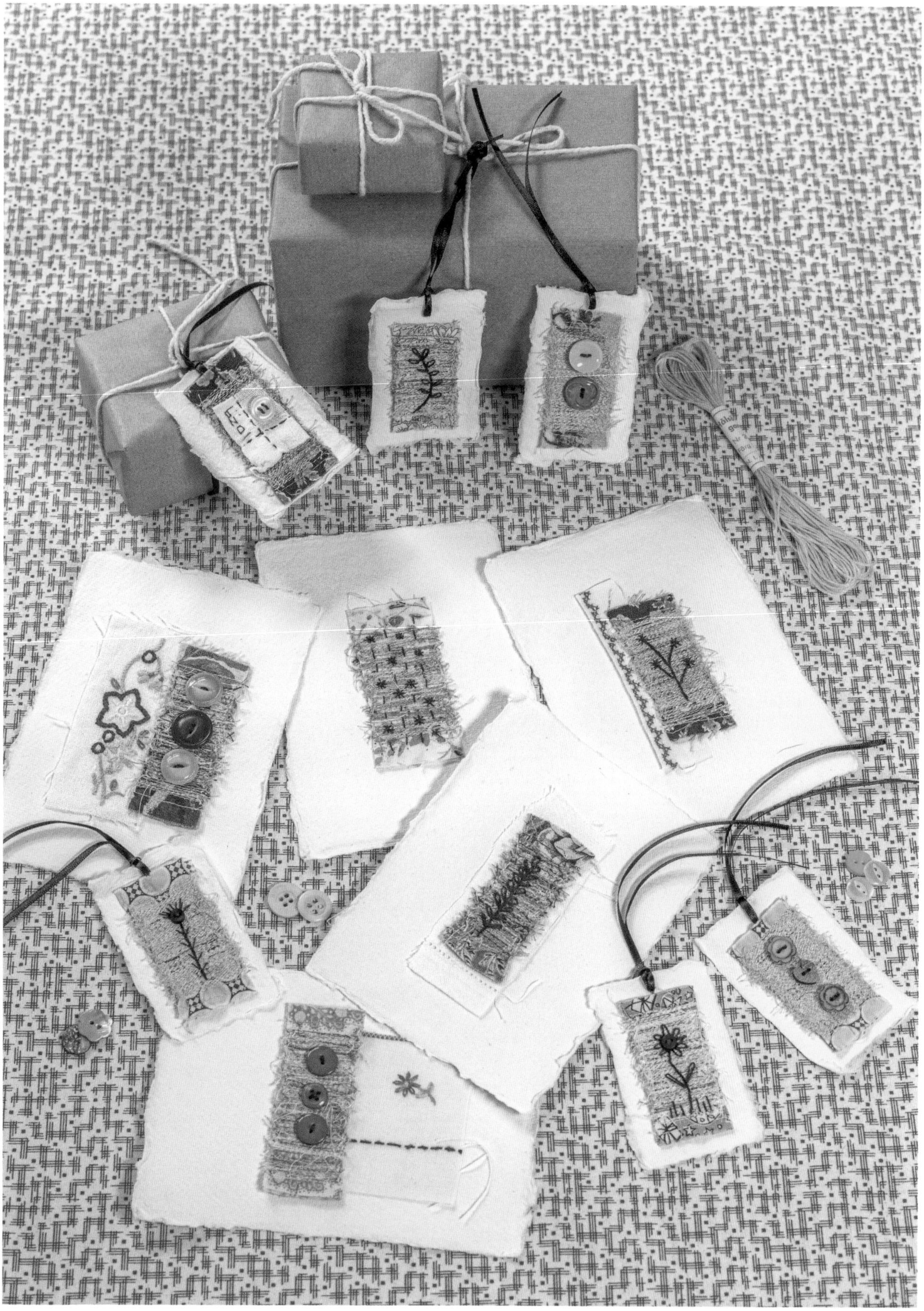

NOTECARDS

REQUIREMENTS

Blank notecards – mine are A6 (4¼ x 5¾in/ 105 x 148mm) in size, and I've used hand-made rag paper as I like the texture

Thread savers

Glue – I used a regular glue stick for the fabrics, and a PVA glue to hold the thread savers in place.

Decoration:

Embroidery thread and embroidery needle – I've used 12wt Coton Perle with a size 6 embroidery needle. I use this combination for hand quilting, so I had both to hand. I like a contrasting colour and I used black here. This means I can use it on all the pieces without chopping and changing.

Buttons – These are often odd vintage buttons that you use to create fun combinations; or, you can use buttons saved from clothes you have cut up (like the shirt on pages 26 and 27).

Fabric and embroidered-cloth scraps – use all the little off-cuts from block and quiltmaking that you've saved. I save the edges of the embroidery that I use in the quilts. I've even saved laundry labels and used these. Choose colours or designs that complement your thread saver.

Tip

If you think your work is too good to use as a notecard, simply frame and keep or give as a gift in its own right.

method

Step One Decorate your thread savers by embroidering them or stitching buttons onto them. For the embroidered thread savers, I've used simple stitches (see the selection opposite). Start your work with a knot that sits on the back of the work, then finish off by hiding the thread between the machine stitches.

Step Two Once the thread savers are decorated they can be glued to the card. If you're also using fabric scraps, stick these down first then glue the thread saver on top. Placement is really up to you – I've positioned my thread savers in the middle of my cards, but making them slightly off-centre or positioning them in a corner looks equally fun.

Step Three Leave to dry, then they're ready to be used.

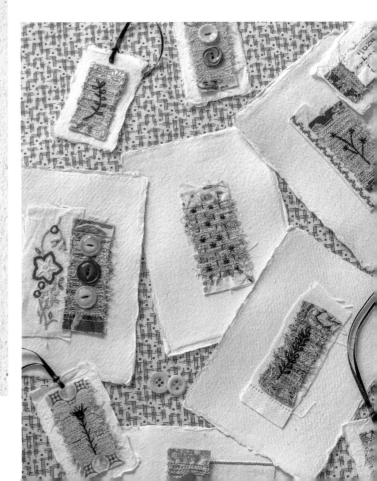

embroidery stitches

Here are the stitches I used for my gift tags and notecards;
however, feel free to use your own favourite stitches for a unique card.

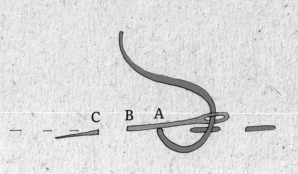

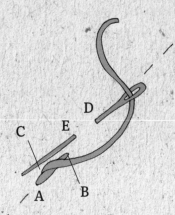

Running stitch – bring the needle up at A, down at B, then up at C. The gap between B and C should be the same size as between A and B. Repeat as desired.

Stem stitch – bring the needle up at A, down at B then up at C, from directly under the stitch but not taking it up through the strands of the thread. Take the needle down a stitch length away, at D, then again bring the needle up from underneath the stitch, at E. Repeat as desired.

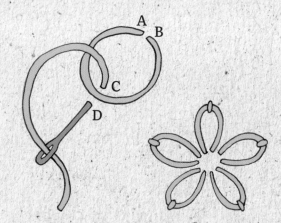

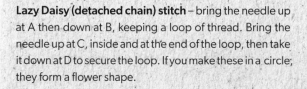

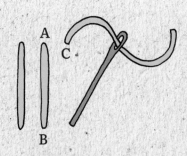

Lazy Daisy (detached chain) stitch – bring the needle up at A then down at B, keeping a loop of thread. Bring the needle up at C, inside and at the end of the loop, then take it down at D to secure the loop. If you make these in a circle, they form a flower shape.

Straight stitch – bring the needle up at A then down at B to make one stitch. Bring the needle up at C to start a new stitch. Making the stitches different lengths can add interest and texture, and stitches can be worked in a circle to form rays.

GIFT TAGS

REQUIREMENTS

Card, for the tags – I cut 2 x 3in (5 x 7.5cm) pieces for each tag. As with the notecards, I've used hand-made rag paper because of I like the lovely textured edges

Thread savers

Narrow ribbon, one 12in (30.5cm) length per gift tag

Chenille needle, size 18 or 22 – I've used this for threading ribbon through the card

Glue – I used a regular glue stick for the fabrics, and a PVA glue to hold the thread savers in place.

Decoration:

<u>Embroidery thread and embroidery needle</u> – I've used 12wt Coton Perle with a size 6 embroidery needle.

<u>Buttons</u> – see the requirements list for the Notecard project on page 164 for more details.

<u>Fabric and embroidered-cloth scraps</u> – as above, see the Notecard project for more details

method

Step One Decorate your thread savers by embroidering them or stitching buttons onto them. For the embroidered thread savers, I've used simple stitches (see the selection on page 165). Start your work with a knot that sits on the back of the work, then finish off by hiding the thread between the machine stitches.

Step Two Once the thread savers are decorated they can be glued to the card pieces. If you're also using fabric scraps, stick these down first then glue the thread saver on top. I've positioned my thread savers in the middle of each gift tag. Leave to dry.

Step Three Fold the ribbon in half, then thread the folded end through the eye of the chenille needle. Pierce a small hole in the top of the card with the threaded needle, about ⅜in (1cm) down from the edge. Wiggle the needle if the hole is not quite big enough. Pull through the loop of ribbon on the needle, remove the needle then take the tail ends of the ribbon through the loop and draw up. You can knot the ends of the ribbon together if you wish.

Templates

Digital templates

These templates are also available to download free from the Bookmarked Hub website:

www.bookmarkedhub.com

Search for this book by title or ISBN; the files can be found under 'Book Extras'.

Membership of the Bookmarked online community is free.

The following templates are provided at 100% scale. Note that the seam allowances for some templates are not included, and will need to be added where necessary. For templates that have the letter 'R' included in the name, this stands for 'reflect' and means you will need to flip the template to create a mirror image. All the templates in the book feature a grainline arrow, which should match the fabric grainline before the shapes are cut out.

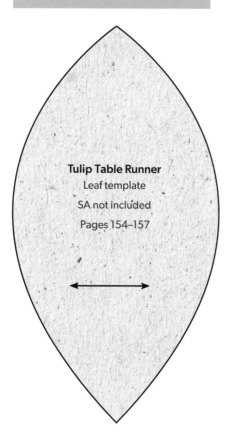

Tulip Table Runner
Leaf template
SA not included
Pages 154–157

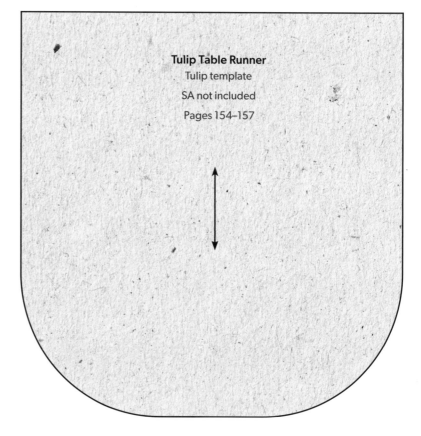

Tulip Table Runner
Tulip template
SA not included
Pages 154–157

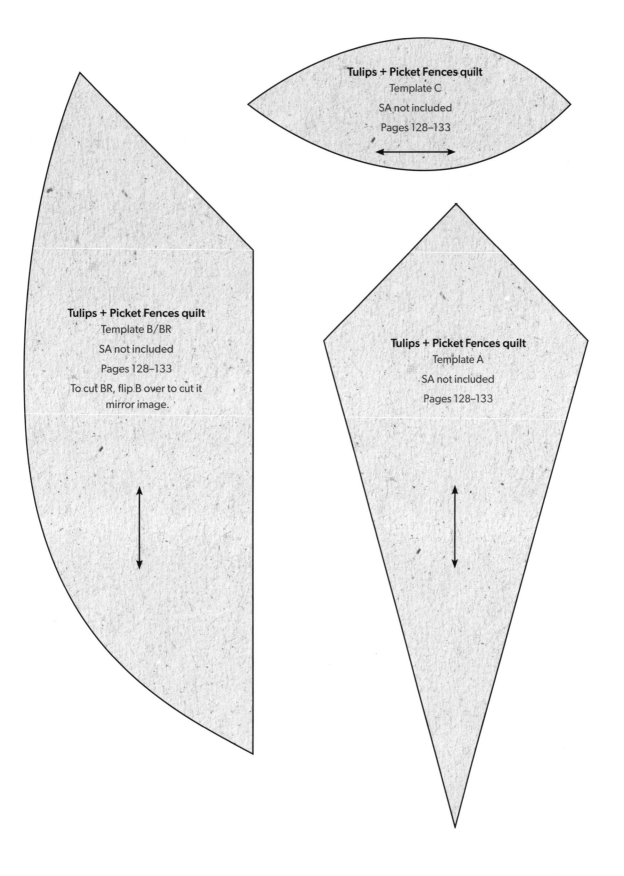

Tulips + Picket Fences quilt
Template C
SA not included
Pages 128–133

Tulips + Picket Fences quilt
Template B/BR
SA not included
Pages 128–133
To cut BR, flip B over to cut it mirror image.

Tulips + Picket Fences quilt
Template A
SA not included
Pages 128–133

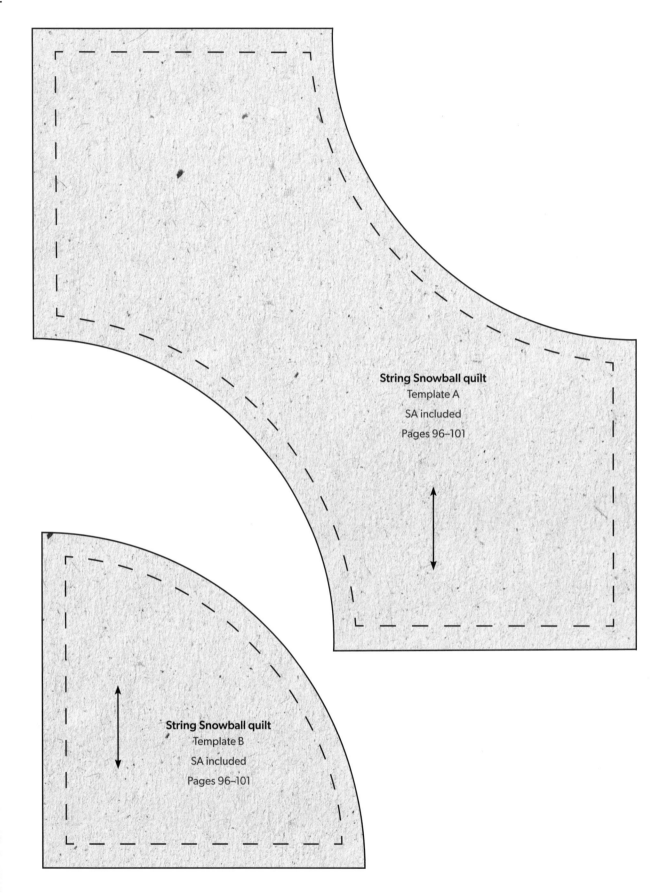

String Snowball quilt
Template A
SA included
Pages 96–101

String Snowball quilt
Template B
SA included
Pages 96–101

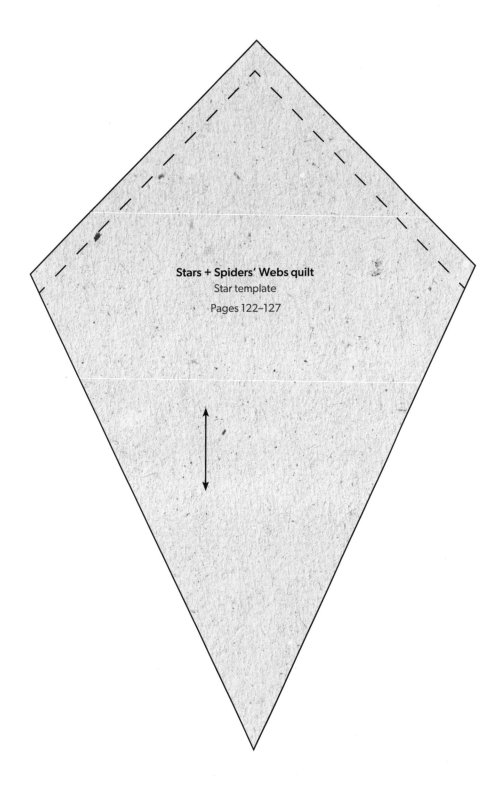

Stars + Spiders' Webs quilt
Star template
Pages 122–127

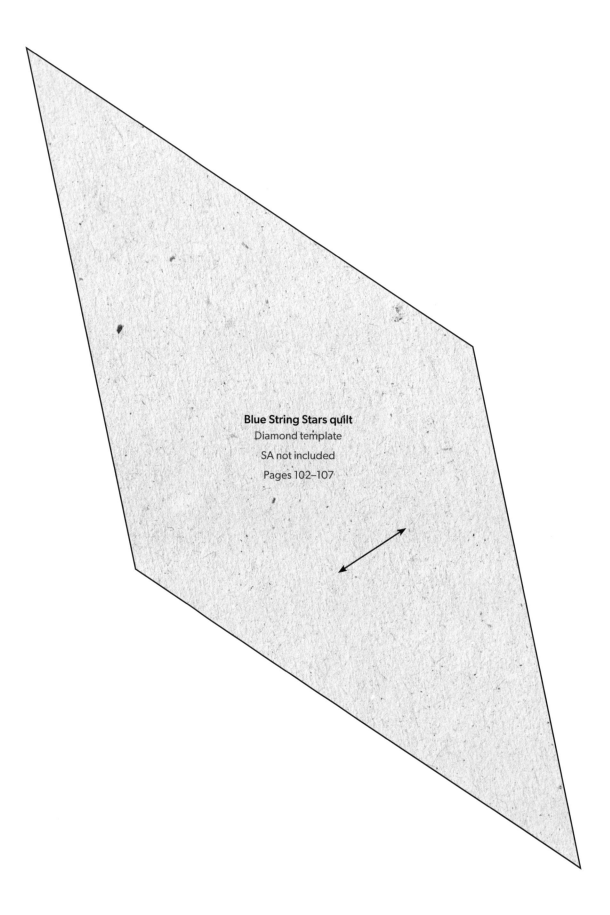

Blue String Stars quilt
Diamond template
SA not included
Pages 102–107

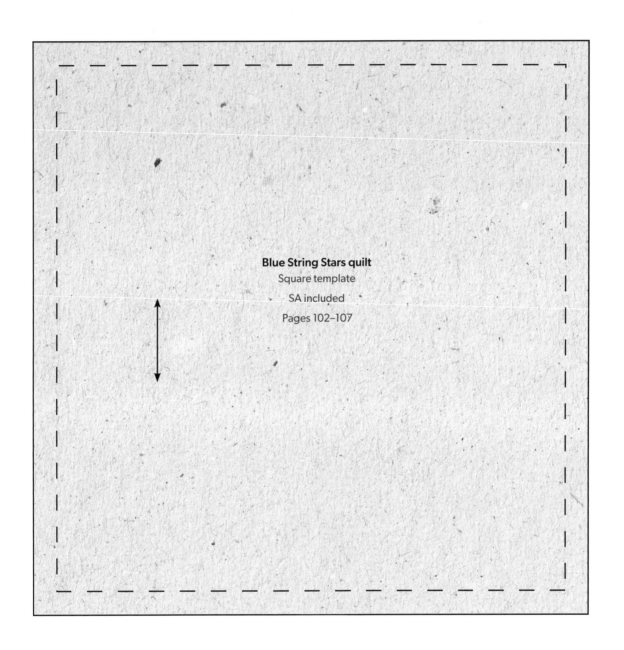

Blue String Stars quilt
Square template
SA included
Pages 102–107

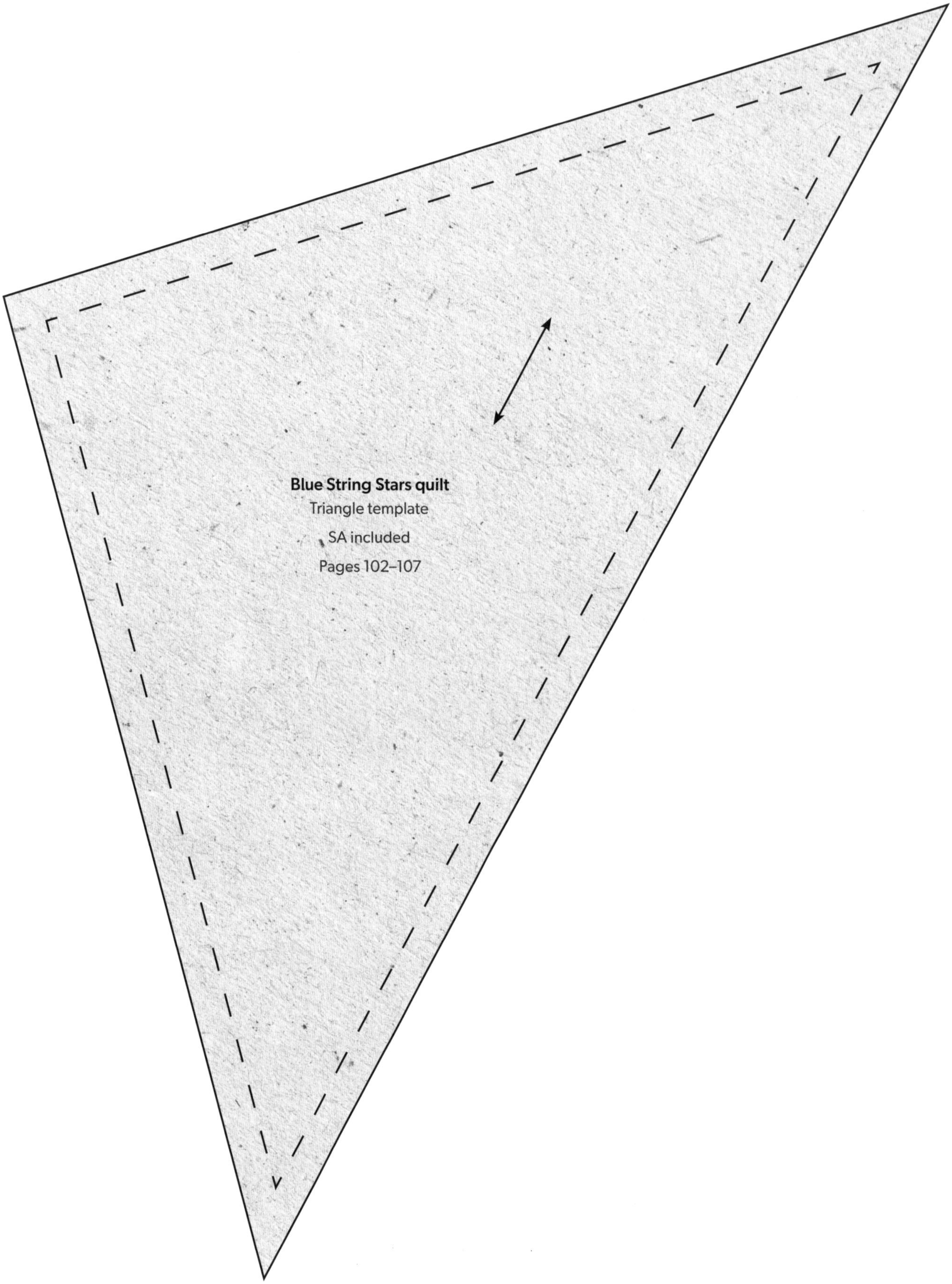

Blue String Stars quilt
Triangle template
SA included
Pages 102–107

Amish Wave
Wave template
Pages 70 and 71

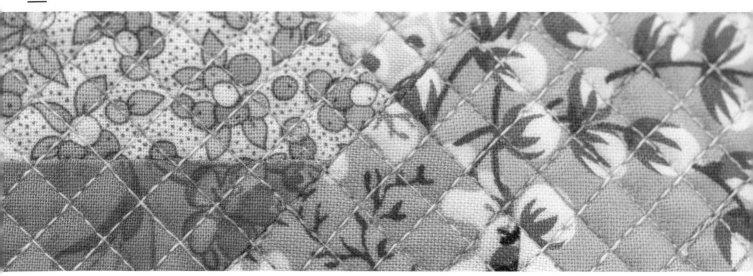

First published in 2024
Search Press Limited
Wellwood, North Farm Road,
Tunbridge Wells, Kent TN2 3DR

Text and templates copyright © Carolyn Forster, 2024

Photographs by Mark Davison for Search Press Studios
Styling by Lisa Brown
Photographs and design copyright © Search Press Ltd. 2024

Illustrations by Bess Harding
copyright © Search Press Ltd. 2024

ISBN: 978-1-80092-082-8
ebook ISBN: 978-1-80093-075-9

SUPPLIERS
For details of suppliers, please visit the Search Press website: www.searchpress.com

ABOUT THE AUTHOR
To see more of Carolyn's work, visit:
– her website: www.carolynforster.co.uk
– her Instagram page, via @quiltingonthego

DIGITAL TEMPLATES
The templates in this book are also available to download free from the Bookmarked Hub website: www.bookmarkedhub.com
Search for this book by title or ISBN; the files can be found under 'Book Extras'. Membership of the Bookmarked online community is free.

IMPERIAL + METRIC CONVERSIONS
The projects in this book have been made using imperial measurements, and the metric equivalents provided have been calculated following standard conversion practices. The metric measurements are often rounded to the nearest 0.25cm for ease of use except in rare circumstances; however, if you need more exact measurements, there are a number of excellent online converters that you can use. Always use either metric or imperial measurements, not a combination of both.

FSC
www.fsc.org
MIX
Paper | Supporting responsible forestry
FSC® C020056